Buckle Down™

Ohio Mathematics

Level 6

3rd Edition

This book belongs to: _____

Buckle Down
Publishing
A Haights Cross Communications Company

Helping your schoolhouse meet the standards of the statehouse™

ISBN 0-7836-4077-3

Catalog #3BDOH06MM01   6 7 8 9 10

Senior Editor: Daniel J. Smith; Project Editor: Jane Mason; Editors: Scott Johanningmeier, Lynn Tauro; Production Editor: Michael Hankes; Cover design: Christina Nantz; Production Director: Jennifer Booth; Art Director: Chris Wolf; Graphic Designer: Beth Oxler; Composition: Wyndham Books.

Cover image: © Steve Cole/Photodisc/Getty Images

TABLE OF CONTENTS

Introduction

Math is all around you. Take this book as an example. Math was used to calculate the margins and the number of pages needed. Math was used to decide where to put tables and other pieces of art. Math was even used to make the illustration on the cover. (And, of course, math was used to write the contents of this book.) Take a look around your classroom—the walls, the pencil sharpener, the windows, and even the plants you see relate in some way to math. You probably use math all the time without even knowing it.

This book will help you practice the math skills that you need in your everyday life, as well as in school. As with anything else, the more you practice these skills, the better you will get at applying them.

Testwise Strategies™

The best way to get a good score on any math test is to learn the math. But there are some other things you can do that may help you get the best possible score using the math you know.

Tip 1: On test day, stay relaxed and confident.

Before you take a test, remind yourself that you are well-prepared and are going to do well. You have good reason to feel confident. If you feel anxious before or during a test, take several slow, deep breaths to relax.

Tip 2: Find the technique that works best for you.

Once you are told to begin, take a quick flip through the test. Start with the easy questions and save the more difficult questions for the end. Before you hand in the test, take a final flip. Make sure you have answered all the questions and have checked your answers for careless mistakes.

Tip 3: Know when to guess.

If you aren't sure of the answer to a multiple-choice question, eliminate any answers you know are wrong, then choose the best answer remaining. Your first choice is often correct, so only change your answers if you are sure of the correction.

Tip 4: Answer short-answer and extended-response questions completely.

When answering short-answer and extended-response questions, show all your work to receive as many points as possible. Write neatly enough that your calculations will be easy to follow. Make your answer easy to see by circling it.

Tip 5: Keep a positive attitude toward math.

Some students tell themselves, "I am never going to need this," or, "I don't have a mathematical mind." Don't tell yourself that you **never**, **don't**, **can't**, or **won't** when you speak about math. Remove those words from your vocabulary. Look for your strengths rather than reinforcing what you think you can't or won't do.

Number,
Number Sense,
and Operations

You've heard of the Great Pyramid in Egypt, haven't you? It was built about 4,500 years ago. People worked on it in groups of 100,000 at a time. It contains approximately two million stone blocks that weigh about 2.5 tons each. The pyramid is about 450 feet tall and its base covers 13 acres.

What do all of these facts have in common? For one, they all include numbers: *4,500* years, groups of *100,000*, *two million* stone blocks, *2.5* tons, *450* feet, and *13* acres. But what's more important is that these facts all require you to use your number sense—your ability to understand numbers.

In this unit, you will use your number sense to review different ways of representing numbers. You will also compare and order integers, fractions, mixed numbers, decimals, and percents. Finally, you will use computation to estimate and solve various types of problems.

In This Unit

Whole Numbers and
   Integers

Fractions, Decimals,
   and Percents

Estimation and Problem
   Solving

Ratio, Proportion, and
   Percent

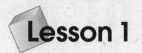

Lesson 1

Whole Numbers and Integers

In this lesson, you will add, subtract, multiply, and divide whole numbers and integers. You will also review multiples, factors, exponents, and prime factorization.

Computation with Whole Numbers

Whole numbers are the counting numbers and zero. Here is the set of whole numbers: {0, 1, 2, 3, . . .}.

Addition

A **sum** is the result of adding two or more numbers. The numbers to be added are called **addends**. Line up the addends vertically by place value. Remember to regroup when necessary.

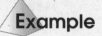 **Example**

Add: 112 + 93

$$\begin{array}{r} 1 \\ 112 \\ + 93 \\ \hline 205 \end{array} \quad \begin{array}{l} \leftarrow\ \textbf{addends} \\ \\ \leftarrow\ \textbf{sum} \end{array}$$

Therefore, 112 + 93 = 205.

Subtraction

A **difference** is the result of subtracting one number from another number. Line up the numbers vertically by place value. Remember to borrow and rename when necessary.

 **Example**

Subtract: 7,389 − 2,928

$$\begin{array}{r} 6\ 13 \\ 7\!\!\!\diagup,\!389 \\ - 2,928 \\ \hline 4,461 \end{array} \quad \leftarrow\ \textbf{difference}$$

Therefore, 7,389 − 2,928 = 4,461.

4

Multiplication

A **product** is the result of multiplying two or more numbers. The numbers that you multiply are called **factors**. Line up the factors vertically by place value. Remember to regroup when necessary.

Example

Multiply: 28 • 13

$$
\begin{array}{r}
{\scriptstyle 2} \\
28 \\
\times\ 13 \\
\hline
{\scriptstyle 1}84 \\
+\ \ 280 \\
\hline
364 \\
\end{array}
$$

factors

product

Therefore, 28 • 13 = 364.

Division

A **quotient** is the answer to a division problem. The number to be divided is called the **dividend**. The number you divide by is called the **divisor**. The **remainder (R)** is the amount that is left over. It must always be smaller than the divisor. A dividend is **divisible** by a divisor when the quotient has a remainder of 0 (R = 0).

Example

Divide: 279 ÷ 23

$$
\begin{array}{r}
12 \quad\leftarrow \text{quotient} \\
\text{divisor} \rightarrow 23\overline{)279} \quad\leftarrow \text{dividend} \\
-\ 23\downarrow \\
\hline
49 \\
-\ 46 \\
\hline
3 \quad\leftarrow \text{remainder} \\
\end{array}
$$

Therefore, 279 ÷ 23 = 12 R3.

Practice

Directions: For Numbers 1 through 12, add, subtract, multiply, or divide.

1. 1,035 + 97 = _1,132_

2. 1,562 − 547 = _1,015_

3. 76 • 12 = _130_

4. 130 ÷ 18 = _400_

5. 3,199 + 837 = _4,036_

6. 953 − 374 = ?
   A. 571
   B. 579
   C. 581
   D. 589

7. 903 • 50 = _953_

8. 392 ÷ 7 = _399_

9. 197 + 871 + 246 = _182_

10. 1,012 − 55 = _155_

11. 142 • 36 = _136_

12. 3,090 ÷ 42 = ?
    A. 71 R8
    B. 73 R24
    C. 74 R18
    D. 75 R40

Computation with Integers

Integers are the counting numbers, their opposites, and zero. Here is the set of integers: $\{\ldots, -3, -2, -1, 0, 1, 2, 3, \ldots\}$.

Addition

The sum of two positive integers is positive.

$$(+) + (+) = + \qquad\qquad 13 + 8 = 21$$

The sum of two negative integers is negative.

$$(-) + (-) = - \qquad\qquad -6 + (-11) = -17$$

The sum of one positive and one negative integer will have the sign of the number with the greater absolute value.

$$(+) + (-) = + \text{ or } - \qquad\qquad 10 + (-5) = 5$$
$$2 + (-14) = -12$$

$$(-) + (+) = + \text{ or } - \qquad\qquad -4 + 17 = 13$$
$$-22 + 15 = -7$$

Subtraction

The difference of two positive integers, two negative integers, or one positive and one negative integer can be either positive or negative.

$$(+) - (+) = + \text{ or } - \qquad\qquad 18 - 3 = 15$$
$$5 - 7 = -2$$

$$(-) - (-) = + \text{ or } - \qquad\qquad -9 - (-14) = 5$$
$$-20 - (-6) = -14$$

$$(+) - (-) = + \qquad\qquad 16 - (-1) = 17$$
$$(-) - (+) = - \qquad\qquad -13 - 8 = -21$$

TIP: To subtract an integer, you add its opposite.

Multiplication and division

The product or quotient of two positive integers is positive.

$(+) \bullet (+) = +$ $2 \bullet 3 = 6$

$(+) \div (+) = +$ $15 \div 5 = 3$

The product or quotient of two negative integers is positive.

$(-) \bullet (-) = +$ $-5 \bullet (-6) = 30$

$(-) \div (-) = +$ $-49 \div (-7) = 7$

The product or quotient of one positive and one negative integer is negative.

$(+) \bullet (-) = -$ $4 \bullet (-8) = -32$

$(-) \bullet (+) = -$ $-7 \bullet 11 = -77$

$(+) \div (-) = -$ $45 \div (-9) = -5$

$(-) \div (+) = -$ $-18 \div 6 = -3$

Real-life situations

Integers can be used for computation in real-life situations. Some keywords that indicate positive integers are *gained*, *increased*, *rose*, *above*, *more*, and *up*. Some keywords that indicate negative integers are *lost*, *decreased*, *dropped*, *below*, *less*, and *down*.

Example

On the first five plays from scrimmage, the Buckeyes gained 6 yards, lost 2 yards, gained 13 yards, gained 1 yard, and lost 7 yards. What was the Buckeyes' net gain or loss?

The following integers represent the Buckeyes' gains and losses.

$6, -2, 13, 1, -7$

Add the integers above to find the net gain or loss.

$$6 + (-2) + 13 + 1 + (-7) = 6 - 2 + 13 + 1 - 7$$
$$= 11$$

The Buckeyes' net gain was 11 yards.

Practice

Directions: For Numbers 1 through 10, add, subtract, multiply, or divide.

1. $6 + (-19) =$ __-7__

2. $20 - (-8) =$ __12__

3. $15 - 18 =$ __-3__

4. $-54 \div 9 =$ __-6__

5. $-7 \cdot (-5) =$ __35__

6. $-2 - (-15) =$ __-17__

7. $-11 + (-23) =$ __-34__

8. $-9 + 18 =$ __27__

9. $-10 \cdot 5 =$ __53__

10. $48 \div 3 =$ __16__

Directions: For Numbers 11 and 12, add or subtract the integers used in real-life situations.

11. The Buckeyes started with the ball on their 20-yard line. On the first play, they lost 12 yards, then they advanced 15 yards, then they lost 3 yards, and finally gained 17. What yard line are the Buckeyes on now?

    -12, 15, 3, 71-

    71-

    10th -16
          -11

           5
        + 5   -13
          ---   -5
           8   ---
                  8

12. Peter got in the elevator on the 10th floor. He rode up 6 floors, then down 11 floors, up 8, and finally down 5. What floor is he on now?

    8th floor

Multiples and Factors

Multiples of a number are the products that result from multiplying the number by each of the whole numbers (0, 1, 2, 3, 4, and so on).

 **Example**

What are the first five multiples of 6?

Multiply 6 by each of the first five whole numbers.

$$6 \cdot 0 = \mathbf{0}$$
$$6 \cdot 1 = \mathbf{6}$$
$$6 \cdot 2 = \mathbf{12}$$
$$6 \cdot 3 = \mathbf{18}$$
$$6 \cdot 4 = \mathbf{24}$$

The first five multiples of 6 are 0, 6, 12, 18, and 24.

A number that is a multiple of two or more numbers is a **common multiple** of those numbers. (Zero is **not** considered a common multiple.) The smallest common multiple of two or more numbers is called their **least common multiple (LCM)**.

Example

What is the LCM of 6 and 8?

multiples of 6: 0, 6, 12, 18, **24**, 30, 36, 42, **48**, 54, . . .

multiples of 8: 0, 8, 16, **24**, 32, 40, **48**, 56, 64, 72, . . .

The numbers 24 and 48 are the first two common multiples of 6 and 8. The least common multiple of 6 and 8 is **24**.

Factors of a number divide that number evenly (remainder of 0). A number is divisible by all its factors.

**Example**

What are the factors of 24?

Find the numbers that divide 24 evenly.

$$24 \div 1 = 24$$
$$24 \div 2 = 12$$
$$24 \div 3 = 8$$
$$24 \div 4 = 6$$
$$24 \div 6 = 4$$
$$24 \div 8 = 3$$
$$24 \div 12 = 2$$
$$24 \div 24 = 1$$

The factors of 24 are 1, 2, 3, 4, 6, 8, 12, and 24.

A number that is a factor of two or more numbers is a **common factor** of those numbers. The largest common factor of two or more numbers is called their **greatest common factor (GCF)**.

**Example**

What is the GCF of 24 and 42?

factors of 24: **1**, **2**, **3**, 4, **6**, 8, 12, and 24

factors of 42: **1**, **2**, **3**, **6**, 7, 14, 21, and 42

The numbers 1, 2, 3, and 6 are the common factors of 24 and 42. The greatest common factor of 24 and 42 is **6**.

Practice

Directions: For Numbers 1 through 4, list the first 10 multiples.

1. multiples of 4: 4, 8, 12, 16, 20, 24, (28), 32, 36, 40

2. multiples of 7: 7, 14, 21, (28), 35, 42, 49, 56, (63), 70

3. multiples of 9: 9, 18, 27, (36), 45, 54, (63), (72), 81, 90

4. multiples of 12: 12, 24, (36), 48, 60, (72), 84, 96, 108, 120

$$\begin{array}{r} 12 \\ \times\ 9 \\ \hline 108 \end{array}$$

5. What is the LCM of 4 and 7? 28   4, 8, 12, 16, 20, 24, 28, 32, 36,
                                       7, 14, 21, 28, 35, 42

6. What is the LCM of 7 and 9? 63

7. What is the LCM of 9 and 12? 72, 36

Directions: For Numbers 8 through 11, list all the factors.

8. factors of 5: 1, 2, 3, (5)

9. factors of 10: 1, 2, 5, 10

10. factors of 17: (1), 17

11. factors of 102: (1),

12. What is the GCF of 5 and 10? 5

13. What is the GCF of 10 and 17? 1

14. What is the GCF of 17 and 102? _____

Exponents

An **exponent** shows how many times a **base number** occurs as a factor. Exponents show repeated multiplication.

When working with exponents, remember that any base number (except zero) with zero as the exponent equals 1. (0^0 is not defined.) Also, any base number with 1 as the exponent equals the base number.

◢ Example

What is the value of 3^5?

The exponent (^{5}) shows that the base number (3) occurs as a factor 5 times.

exponent
$$\downarrow$$
$$3^5 = 3 \cdot 3 \cdot 3 \cdot 3 \cdot 3 = 243$$
$$\uparrow$$
base number

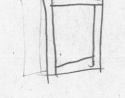

Therefore, $3^5 = 243$.

◢ Example

How is 625 written using exponents?

First, write 625 using repeated multiplication of the same factor.

$$625 = 5 \cdot 5 \cdot 5 \cdot 5$$

Next, write the factor as the base number and the number of times you multiplied that factor as the exponent.

$$5 \cdot 5 \cdot 5 \cdot 5 = 5^4$$

Therefore, $625 = 5^4$.

➥ **TIP:** Exponents are called **powers** when you read them. An exponent of 2 can be read as "to the second power" or "squared," and an exponent of 3 can be read as "to the third power" or "cubed."

Practice

Directions: For Numbers 1 through 7, write the expression as the factors of the base number and then evaluate.

1. $9^3 =$ _____ = _____

2. $15^0 =$ _____ = _____

3. $10^2 =$ _____ = _____

4. $6^4 =$ _____ = _____

5. $12^1 =$ _____ = _____

6. $2^7 =$ _____ = _____

7. $4^5 =$ _____ = _____

Directions: For Numbers 8 through 11, write each number first using repeated multiplication of the same factor, then using exponents.

8. $512 =$ _____ = _____

9. $49 =$ _____ = _____

10. $125 =$ _____ = _____

11. $10,000 =$ _____ = _____

Prime Factorization

Prime factorization is a way of expressing a composite number as the product of prime numbers. A **prime number** has only two factors: 1 and the number. A **composite number** has at least three factors. Remember, 0 and 1 are neither prime nor composite numbers. You can use a **factor tree** to determine the prime factorization of a composite number.

◢ Example

What is the prime factorization of 504?

Write the number 504. Write a prime factor under the left branch and circle it. Write the composite factor under the right branch. Repeat this process under each composite number until you have two prime numbers at the bottom of the tree. The prime factorization is the product of all the circled numbers.

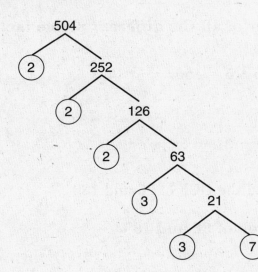

The prime factorization of 504 is 2 • 2 • 2 • 3 • 3 • 7 or $2^3 • 3^2 • 7$.

Note: There is more than one way to make a factor tree. In the first step of this example, you could have divided by 3 or 7 instead of by 2. The order in which you find the prime factors doesn't matter. However, when you list the prime factors in your answer, list them in order from least to greatest.

Prime factorization can be used to find the least common multiple (LCM) and the greatest common factor (GCF) of two or more numbers.

Example

Use prime factorization to find the LCM of 75 and 90.

Step 1: Find the prime factorizations of 75 and 90.

$$75 = 3 \cdot 5^2$$

$$90 = 2 \cdot 3^2 \cdot 5$$

Step 2: Circle the highest power of all the *different* prime factors of both numbers.

$$75 = 3 \cdot \boxed{5^2}$$

$$90 = \boxed{2} \cdot \boxed{3^2} \cdot 5$$

Step 3: Multiply the highest power of all the *different* prime factors from Step 2.

$$2 \cdot 3^2 \cdot 5^2 = 2 \cdot 3 \cdot 3 \cdot 5 \cdot 5 = 450$$

The LCM of 75 and 90 is **450**.

Example

Use prime factorization to find the GCF of 96 and 180.

Step 1: Find the prime factorization of 96 and 180.

$$96 = 2^5 \cdot 3$$

$$180 = 2^2 \cdot 3^2 \cdot 5$$

Step 2: Circle the lowest power of the *common* prime factors of both numbers.

$$96 = 2^5 \cdot \boxed{3}$$

$$180 = \boxed{2^2} \cdot 3^2 \cdot 5$$

Step 3: Multiply the lowest power of the *common* prime factors from Step 2.

$$2^2 \cdot 3 = 2 \cdot 2 \cdot 3 = 12$$

The GCF of 96 and 180 is **12**.

Practice

1. Draw a factor tree for 45.

   The prime factorization of 45 is _____.

2. Draw a factor tree for 800.

   The prime factorization of 800 is _____.

3. What is the LCM of 45 and 800? _____

4. What is the GCF of 45 and 800? _____

5. Draw a factor tree for 120.

The prime factorization of 120 is _____.

6. Draw a factor tree for 1,260.

The prime factorization of 1,260 is _____.

7. What is the LCM of 120 and 1,260? _____

8. What is the GCF of 120 and 1,260? _____

Order of Operations

When simplifying an expression, you must follow the correct order of operations. The following example shows the steps needed to simplify an expression.

 **Example**

Simplify the following expression.

$20 + 7 \cdot (4 \div 2) - 5^2$

Step 1: Simplify all expressions in parentheses.

$(4 \div 2) = 2$

$20 + 7 \cdot \mathbf{2} - 5^2$

Step 2: Simplify exponents.

$5^2 = 25$

$20 + 7 \cdot 2 - \mathbf{25}$

Step 3: Perform all multiplication and division in order from left to right.

$7 \cdot 2 = 14$

$20 + \mathbf{14} - 25$

Step 4: Perform all addition and subtraction in order from left to right.

$20 + 14 = 34$

$\mathbf{34} - 25 = 9$

The expression simplifies to 9.

Practice

Directions: For Numbers 1 through 6, use the correct order of operations to simplify each expression.

1. $12 - 1 \bullet 6 \div 3 \bullet 2 + 1 = $ _____

2. $12 - 1 \bullet (6 \div 3) \bullet (2 + 1) = $ _____

3. $(12 \bullet 6) \div (3 \bullet 2) + 1 - 1 = $ _____

4. $12 \bullet (6 - 1) \div 3 \bullet 2^2 + 1 = $ _____

5. $1 + 12 \bullet 6 \div 3 \bullet 2^2 - 1 = $ _____

6. $12 \bullet 6 \div (3 \bullet 2)^2 = $ _____

Achievement Practice

1. What is the GCF of 72 and 84?

   A.   6

   B.   8

   C. 12

   D. 18

2. Which calculation should you perform first to simplify the following expression?

   $$6^2 \div 3 \cdot 2 + (4 - 3)$$

   A. $3 \cdot 2$

   B. $2 + 4$

   C. $4 - 3$

   D. $6^2 \div 3$

3. What is the value of 7^3?

   A.   21

   B.   343

   C. 1,029

   D. 2,187

4. Maurice took 8 steps forward, 3 steps backward, 12 steps forward, 7 steps backward, and 1 step forward. What is the net amount of steps Maurice took forward or backward?

   A. 11 steps forward

   B. 7 steps forward

   C. 9 steps backward

   D. 15 steps backward

5. Add: −45 + 19

   A. 64

   B. 26

   C. −26

   D. −64

6. What is the prime factorization of 60?

   A. 5 • 6

   B. $2 \cdot 3^3$

   C. 3 • 4 • 5

   D. $2^2 \cdot 3 \cdot 5$

7. Divide: 689 ÷ 23

   A. 25 R14

   B. 29 R22

   C. 30 R19

   D. 31 R6

8. Which of the following is equal to 512?

   A. 2^8

   B. 4^5

   C. 6^4

   D. 8^3

9. Simplify the following expression.

   $$4 \cdot (-8 - 4) \div (9 + 7)$$

   A. 3

   B. 1

   C. −1

   D. −3

10. Which list shows only multiples of 9?

    A. 18, 36, 44

    B. 24, 45, 54

    C. 27, 36, 63

    D. 36, 54, 75

11. Subtract: 174 − 88

    A. 86

    B. 96

    C. 104

    D. 114

12. What is the prime factorization of 350?

    A. $2 \cdot 5^2 \cdot 7$

    B. $2^2 \cdot 3 \cdot 9$

    C. 2 • 5 • 35

    D. 5 • 7 • 10

13. Which list shows the factors of 32?

    A. 1, 2, 4, 6, 12, 32

    B. 1, 2, 4, 8, 16, 32

    C. 1, 2, 3, 4, 8, 12, 32

    D. 1, 2, 3, 4, 6, 8, 16, 32

14. Multiply: $-17 \cdot (-6)$

    A. 112

    B. 102

    C. -102

    D. -112

15. What are the LCM and the GCF of 18 and 24?

    LCM: _____

    GCF: _____

16. What is the prime factorization of 2,268? Show your work.

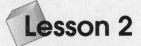

Lesson 2
Fractions, Decimals, and Percents

In this lesson, you will compute with and review the relationships between fractions, decimals, and percents. You will use these relationships to compare and order integers, fractions, decimals, and percents, and to find their locations on a number line.

Fractions

A **fraction** is a rational number that can be written in the form of $\frac{a}{b}$, where a and b are integers and b does not equal zero. The top number of a fraction is the **numerator**, and the bottom number is the **denominator**. The following rectangle has 3 of its 4 equal parts shaded.

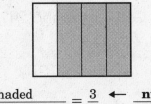

$$\frac{\text{parts shaded}}{\text{total parts in the whole}} = \frac{3}{4} \quad\begin{matrix}\leftarrow \textbf{numerator} \\ \leftarrow \textbf{denominator}\end{matrix}$$

The fraction of the rectangle that is shaded can be written as $\frac{3}{4}$. You can also say that 3 parts of the rectangle are shaded. Each part is $\frac{1}{4}$ of the rectangle.

Example

What fraction of the following state shapes are shaded?

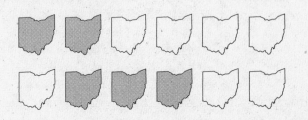

Five shapes are shaded. There are a total of 12 shapes. The fraction of shapes that are shaded is $\frac{5}{12}$.

24

Computation with fractions and mixed numbers

Before calculating with a mixed number, you may need to convert the mixed number into an improper fraction. Reduce all answers to lowest terms.

Addition and subtraction

To add or subtract fractions and mixed numbers with the same denominator, simply add or subtract the numerators, and keep the denominator the same.

 **Example**

Subtract: $\frac{9}{10} - \frac{4}{10}$

Subtract the numerators and write the answer in lowest terms.

$$\frac{9}{10} - \frac{4}{10} = \frac{9-4}{10} = \frac{5}{10} = \frac{1}{2}$$

Therefore, $\frac{9}{10} - \frac{4}{10} = \frac{1}{2}$.

To add or subtract fractions and mixed numbers with different denominators, you need to find the least common denominator (LCD).

Example

Add: $\frac{1}{6} + \frac{3}{4}$

Find the LCM of 6 and 4 to use as the LCD for both fractions.

The LCM of 6 and 4 is 12.

Multiply the numerator and denominator of each fraction by the number needed to make each denominator equal to the LCD.

$$\frac{1 \cdot 2}{6 \cdot 2} = \frac{2}{12} \qquad\qquad \frac{3 \cdot 3}{4 \cdot 3} = \frac{9}{12}$$

Add the numerators and write the answer in lowest terms.

$$\frac{2}{12} + \frac{9}{12} = \frac{11}{12}$$

Therefore, $\frac{1}{6} + \frac{3}{4} = \frac{11}{12}$.

Multiplication

It is not necessary to have the same denominator to multiply fractions and mixed numbers. All you need to do is multiply the numerators, multiply the denominators, and then reduce the answer to lowest terms.

▲ Example

Multiply: $\frac{4}{5} \cdot \frac{7}{8}$

Multiply the numerators and the denominators and write the answer in lowest terms.

$$\frac{4 \cdot 7}{5 \cdot 8} = \frac{28}{40} = \frac{7}{10}$$

Therefore, $\frac{4}{5} \cdot \frac{7}{8} = \frac{7}{10}$.

Division

Dividing by a fraction is the same as multiplying by the **reciprocal** of the fraction. To find the reciprocal of a fraction, switch its numerator and denominator. When the dividend is greater than 1 and the divisor is a fraction, the quotient will be larger than the dividend.

▲ Example

Divide: $2\frac{2}{3} \div \frac{4}{9}$

Change the mixed number to an improper fraction.

$$2\frac{2}{3} = \frac{8}{3}$$

Flip the second fraction and change division to multiplication.

$\frac{8}{3} \div \frac{4}{9}$ becomes $\frac{8}{3} \cdot \frac{9}{4}$

Multiply the numerators and the denominators and write the answer in lowest terms.

$$\frac{8 \cdot 9}{3 \cdot 4} = \frac{72}{12} = 6$$

Therefore, $2\frac{2}{3} \div \frac{4}{9} = 6$.

Practice

Directions: For Numbers 1 through 12, add, subtract, multiply, or divide. Make sure your answers are in lowest terms.

1. $\frac{3}{8} - \frac{1}{3} =$ _____

2. $\frac{2}{7} \cdot \frac{3}{4} =$ _____

3. $\frac{1}{12} + \frac{5}{9} =$ _____

4. $8 \div \frac{4}{5} =$ _____

5. $2\frac{8}{13} - 1\frac{3}{5} =$ _____

6. $\frac{1}{4} + \frac{1}{6} = ?$

   A. $\frac{1}{5}$

   B. $\frac{1}{3}$

   C. $\frac{3}{8}$

   D. $\frac{5}{12}$

7. $\frac{5}{6} - \frac{1}{6} =$ _____

8. $5\frac{5}{8} \div 1\frac{3}{4} =$ _____

9. $\frac{2}{3} \div \frac{1}{2} =$ _____

10. $\frac{1}{8} \cdot \frac{1}{2} =$ _____

11. $5\frac{6}{7} + \frac{4}{7} =$ _____

12. $\frac{9}{10} \cdot 10\frac{1}{2} = ?$

   A. $9\frac{9}{20}$

   B. $10\frac{9}{20}$

   C. $10\frac{11}{20}$

   D. $11\frac{2}{3}$

Decimals

A **decimal** is a number form that expresses a whole divided into ten equal parts (ten**ths**), one hundred equal parts (hundred**ths**), one thousand equal parts (thousand**ths**), and so on. The following table shows the place values for the decimals 9.018 and 825.734.

Hundreds	Tens	Ones	Decimal Point	Tenths	Hundredths	Thousandths
		9	.	0	1	8
8	2	5	.	7	3	4

Computation with decimals

You can compute with decimals in a way that is similar to the way you compute with whole numbers.

Addition and subtraction

When adding or subtracting decimals, line up the decimal points. Move the decimal point straight down into the answer. Add or subtract the numbers as you would for whole numbers. Use zeros as placeholders when necessary.

 **Example**

Add: 40.5 + 7.132

$$
\begin{array}{r}
40.5\mathbf{00} \quad \leftarrow \text{ Use zeros as placeholders.} \\
+ \quad 7.132 \\
\hline
47.632
\end{array}
$$

Therefore, 40.5 + 7.132 = 47.632.

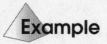 **Example**

Subtract: 24.94 − 3.074

$$
\begin{array}{r}
^{8\,13\,10} \\
24.9\cancel{40} \quad \leftarrow \text{ Use zero as a placeholder.} \\
- \quad 3.074 \\
\hline
21.866
\end{array}
$$

Therefore, 24.94 − 3.074 = 21.866.

Multiplication

Multiply decimals as if they were whole numbers. Then count the number of digits to the right of the decimal point in each factor. Finally, move the decimal point that many places to the left in the product.

 **Example**

Multiply: 245.76 • 4.5

$$
\begin{array}{r}
245.76 \\
\times \quad 4.5 \\
\hline
{\scriptstyle 1 \ \ 1 \ \ \ \ 1} \\
122880 \\
983040 \\
\hline
1,105.920 \\
\end{array}
$$

Therefore, 245.76 • 4.5 = 1,105.92.

Division

If the divisor is a decimal, move the decimal point to the right to make it a whole number. Move the decimal point in the dividend to the right the same number of places. Then divide as if they were whole numbers. Finally, move the decimal point straight up from its new location into the quotient.

 **Example**

Divide: 8.4 ÷ 2.4

$$
\begin{array}{r}
3.5 \\
2.4.\overline{)8.4.0} \\
-\ 7\,2 \\
\hline
1\,2\,0 \\
-\ 1\,2\,0 \\
\hline
0 \\
\end{array}
$$

Therefore, 8.4 ÷ 2.4 = 3.5.

Practice

Directions: For Numbers 1 through 14, add, subtract, multiply, or divide.

1. 0.7 + 5.09 = _____

2. 45.3 • 2.34 = _____

3. 0.24 + 9.842 = _____

4. 26,992 ÷ 2.8 = _____

5. 8.9 − 1.12 = _____

6. 123.09 − 11.1 = _____

7. 3,485 ÷ 0.17 = ?

   A. 20,500

   B. 2,050

   C. 205

   D. 20.5

8. 64.2 • 3.4 = _____

9. 0.03 + 14.7 = _____

10. 20.18 ÷ 0.2 = _____

11. 45.6 • 11.5 = _____

12. 26 − 0.4 = _____

13. 1.8 ÷ 7.2 = _____

14. 3.409 • 0.15 = ?

   A. 511.35

   B. 51.135

   C. 5.1135

   D. 0.51135

Percents

Percent literally means "for each hundred." Percents represent the parts of a whole unit that is divided into 100 equal parts. The following grid represents a whole unit, or 100%. The grid shows that 16 units out of 100 are shaded. Therefore, 16% of the grid is shaded.

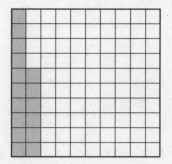

Practice

Directions: For Numbers 1 and 2, determine the percent of the grid that is shaded.

1. _____

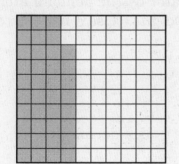

2. _____

Directions: For Numbers 3 and 4, shade in the given percent of each grid.

3. 92%

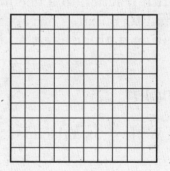

4. 18%

Relating Fractions, Decimals, and Percents

Fractions, decimals, and percents are all ways of representing rational numbers and expressing parts of a whole.

The grid above shows 45 of its 100 parts shaded. As a fraction, this is written $\frac{45}{100}$. As a decimal, it is written 0.45. As a percent, it is written 45%. All three of these, $\frac{45}{100}$, 0.45, and 45% are equivalent expressions. They each represent 45 parts of the whole. The relationships between fractions, decimals, and percents allow us to convert from one form to another.

Converting a fraction to a decimal

To convert a fraction to a decimal, divide the numerator by the denominator until the decimal terminates or repeats a digit or block of digits. (Use a bar, $^{-}$, to show the repeating digit or block of digits.)

Examples

Write $\frac{3}{8}$ as a decimal.

$$
\begin{array}{r}
0.375 \\
8\overline{)3.000} \\
-\,2\,4\!\downarrow \\
\hline
60 \\
-\,56\!\downarrow \\
\hline
40 \\
-\,40 \\
\hline
0
\end{array}
$$

$\frac{3}{8} = 0.375$

Write $\frac{1}{6}$ as a decimal.

$$
\begin{array}{r}
0.166 \\
6\overline{)1.000} \\
-\,6\!\downarrow \\
\hline
40 \\
-\,36\!\downarrow \\
\hline
40 \\
-\,36 \\
\hline
4 \quad \text{(repeating)}
\end{array}
$$

$\frac{1}{6} = 0.1\overline{6}$

Converting a percent to a decimal

To convert a percent to a decimal, remove the percent sign and then move the decimal point two places to the left.

 **Examples**

Write 76% as a decimal.

76% = 0.76

Write 18.5% as a decimal.

18.5% = 0.185

Converting a decimal to a percent

To convert a decimal to a percent, move the decimal point two places to the right and then write the percent sign, %.

 **Examples**

Write 0.065 as a percent.

0.065 = 6.5%

Write 1.09 as a percent.

1.09 = 109%

Converting a fraction to a percent

To convert a fraction to a percent, first divide the numerator by the denominator to find the decimal form. Next, move the decimal point two places to the right and write the percent sign (%).

 **Examples**

Write $\frac{7}{10}$ as a percent.

The decimal form of $\frac{7}{10}$ is 0.7,

so the percent is:

0.7 = 70%

$\frac{7}{10} = 70\%$

Write $\frac{1}{8}$ as a percent.

The decimal form of $\frac{1}{8}$ is 0.125,

so the percent is:

0.125 = 12.5%

$\frac{1}{8} = 12.5\%$

Converting a decimal to a fraction

To convert a decimal to a fraction, write the fraction that you would state if you read the decimal aloud correctly. Then reduce to lowest terms when necessary by dividing the numerator and denominator by the same number. Use the following table of placeholders to help you read the decimal correctly.

Ones	"And"	Tenths	Hundredths	Thousandths
0	.	3	4	
1	.	3	7	5

Examples

Write 0.34 as a fraction.

0.34 is read "thirty-four hundredths," so the fraction is:

$$\frac{34 \div 2}{100 \div 2} = \frac{17}{50}$$

$$0.34 = \frac{17}{50}$$

Write 1.375 as a fraction.

1.375 is read "one and three hundred seventy-five thousandths," so the fraction is:

$$1\frac{375 \div 125}{1{,}000 \div 125} = 1\frac{3}{8}$$

$$1.375 = 1\frac{3}{8}$$

Converting a percent to a fraction

To convert a percent to a fraction, first write the percent as a decimal, then convert the fraction to a decimal. Finally, reduce the fraction to lowest terms when necessary.

Examples

Write 37% as a fraction.

The decimal form of 37% is 0.37, so the fraction is:

$$\frac{37}{100}$$

$$37\% = \frac{37}{100}$$

Write 2.5% as a fraction.

The decimal form of 2.5% is 0.025, so the fraction is:

$$\frac{25 \div 25}{1{,}000 \div 25} = \frac{1}{40}$$

$$2.5\% = \frac{1}{40}$$

 **Practice**

Directions: For Numbers 1 through 6, convert to the given forms.

1. Convert $\frac{6}{15}$ to a: decimal _____ percent _____

2. Convert 0.61 to a: fraction _____ percent _____

3. Convert 29.5% to a: decimal _____ fraction _____

4. Convert $\frac{10}{16}$ to a: decimal _____ percent _____

5. Convert 0.22 to a: fraction _____ percent _____

6. Convert 84% to a: decimal _____ fraction _____

7. Write three equivalent forms (fraction, decimal, and percent) of any rational number.

_____

8. How is 0.035 written as a fraction?

   A. $\frac{1}{40}$

   B. $\frac{1}{400}$

   C. $\frac{7}{200}$

   D. $\frac{7}{2,000}$

9. How is $1\frac{25}{30}$ written as a decimal?

   A. 1.95

   B. $1.8\overline{3}$

   C. 1.65

   D. $1.5\overline{6}$

Comparing and Ordering Different Forms of Numbers

To compare and order integers, fractions, mixed numbers, decimals, and percents, convert all the numbers to the same form.

Example

Compare the numbers and order them from **least** to **greatest**.

$$1\frac{1}{4} \qquad 0.475 \qquad -2 \qquad 20\%$$

Change $1\frac{1}{4}$ and 20% to decimals.

$1\frac{1}{4}$	0.475	-2	20%
becomes	remains	remains	becomes
↓	↓	↓	↓
1.25	0.475	-2	0.2

Now compare the decimals. Write them in order from least to greatest.

$$-2 \qquad 0.2 \qquad 0.475 \qquad 1.25$$

Then write the original numbers in order from least to greatest.

$$-2 \qquad 20\% \qquad 0.475 \qquad 1\frac{1}{4}$$

Example

Write the following numbers in their correct places on the number line.

$$1.6, \ 3\frac{1}{2}, \ 2, \ \frac{4}{5}$$

Each mark on the number line represents $\frac{1}{5}$, or 0.2. Now the numbers can be written in order on the number line.

 **Practice**

Directions: For Numbers 1 through 6, compare the numbers using $<$, $>$, or $=$.

1. $\frac{1}{2}$ _____ 0.50

2. 19% _____ $\frac{9}{50}$

3. 92.5% _____ 0.925

4. 0.36 _____ 33%

5. 1.75 _____ $1\frac{3}{4}$

6. $\frac{2}{5}$ _____ 46%

Directions: For Numbers 7 through 10, write the numbers in order from **least** to **greatest**.

7. $1\frac{5}{8}$ 1.14   2   12% _____

8. 35.5%   −3 $\frac{5}{12}$ 0.306 _____

9. 6% $1\frac{1}{2}$ 0.65 $\frac{1}{15}$ _____

10. 110% $\frac{9}{10}$ 0.195   −1 _____

11. Which list orders the numbers from **greatest** to **least**?

    A. 45.9%, $\frac{1}{2}$, 0.736, $\frac{8}{9}$

    B. 6.41, 200%, 1.85, $\frac{24}{25}$

    C. $\frac{2}{3}$, 0.401, 55%, $\frac{1}{12}$

    D. 7.82, $\frac{4}{7}$, 1.99, 6.45%

12. Which list orders the numbers from **least** to **greatest**?

    A. 2.33, 100%, $\frac{7}{8}$, 0.245

    B. $\frac{3}{10}$, 75%, 4.001, −10

    C. 50%, $2\frac{1}{5}$, 7, 0.99

    D. −5, 6%, 0.986, $1\frac{2}{3}$

Directions: For Numbers 13 and 14, write the numbers in their correct places on the number line.

13. $2\frac{3}{10}$, 1, 3.8, $\frac{3}{5}$

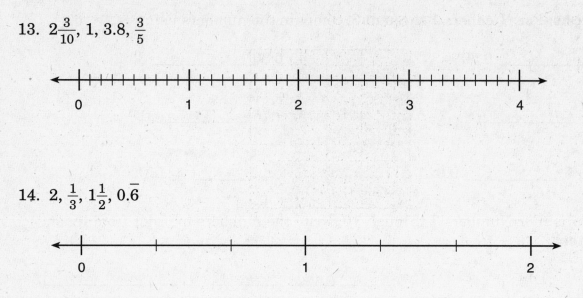

14. 2, $\frac{1}{3}$, $1\frac{1}{2}$, $0.\overline{6}$

15. Write 0.5 in the correct figure under the number line.

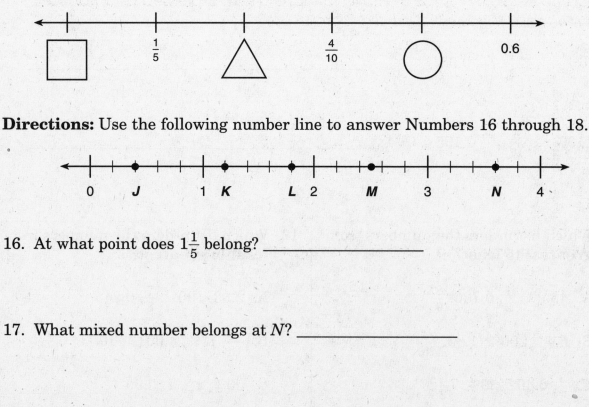

Directions: Use the following number line to answer Numbers 16 through 18.

16. At what point does $1\frac{1}{5}$ belong? _____

17. What mixed number belongs at *N*? _____

18. What decimal belongs at *M*? _____

Achievement Practice

1. What percent of the grid is shaded?

    A. 70%

    B. 74%

    C. 78%

    D. 82%

2. Camille used 0.4 yards of fabric to make a skirt. Expressed as a fraction, how many yards of fabric did Camille use?

    A. $\frac{1}{4}$

    B. $\frac{2}{5}$

    C. $\frac{3}{4}$

    D. $\frac{4}{5}$

3. Which list orders the numbers from **least** to **greatest**?

    A. 3.25, 92%, $\frac{6}{7}$, 0.64

    B. $\frac{4}{9}$, 67%, 6.02, $\frac{1}{2}$

    C. −7, 11%, $4\frac{2}{3}$, 7.157

    D. 80%, $2\frac{1}{5}$, 8, 0.32

4. Multiply:

$$\frac{2}{3} \cdot 17\frac{1}{4}$$

A. $11\frac{1}{2}$

B. $11\frac{1}{4}$

C. $11\frac{5}{12}$

D. $11\frac{7}{12}$

5. Add: $\frac{4}{9} + \frac{1}{6}$

A. $\frac{2}{3}$

B. $\frac{11}{18}$

C. $\frac{1}{3}$

D. $\frac{5}{18}$

6. Divide: $\frac{7}{16} \div \frac{3}{8}$

A. $\frac{1}{16}$

B. $\frac{21}{128}$

C. 1

D. $1\frac{1}{6}$

7. Multiply: $84.7 \cdot 0.68$

A. 10.258

B. 57.596

C. 102.58

D. 575.96

8. Divide: $4.85 \div 0.05$

A. 89

B. 93

C. 97

D. 101

9. Add: $20.18 + 19.9$

A. 39.98

B. 40.08

C. 40.18

D. 40.28

10. How is $\frac{2}{8}$ written as a decimal?

A. 0.25

B. 0.28

C. 0.32

D. 0.35

11. What fraction of the circle is **not** shaded?

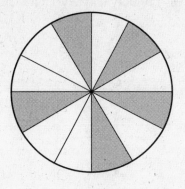

    A. $\frac{7}{12}$

    B. $\frac{6}{12}$

    C. $\frac{5}{12}$

    D. $\frac{4}{12}$

12. How is 0.105 written as a percent?

    A.   0.105%

    B.   1.05%

    C. 10.5%

    D. 105%

13. Which list orders the numbers from **greatest** to **least**?

    A. 23%, 0, $\frac{8}{9}$, 5.22

    B. $1\frac{6}{7}$, 1.25, 40%, $\frac{4}{11}$

    C. −2.2, $\frac{5}{4}$, 0.88, 10

    D. 0.1, 100%, −3.5, $5\frac{3}{4}$

14. Each of four carpenters had 30 days to build 100 bird feeders for the Ohio state bird, the cardinal. After 15 days, they had completed the following parts of their jobs.

    Brian: 75%

    Kate: 0.76

    Patrick: $\frac{7}{12}$

    Loren: $\frac{3}{4}$

    Who built the greatest number of feeders?

    A. Brian

    B. Kate

    C. Patrick

    D. Loren

15. How is 92% written as a decimal and as a fraction in lowest terms?

    decimal: _____

    fraction: _____

16. In the box below, subtract 0.625 from 0.65. Show your work.

Lesson 3

Estimation and Problem Solving

In this lesson, you will review estimating and problem-solving steps that will make solving real-life problems easier.

Estimation

Estimation is a good way to make sure your answer to a problem is reasonable. One estimation strategy commonly used is **rounding**. When rounding, it is important to know place value.

Rounding whole numbers and decimals

When rounding whole numbers and decimals, follow these steps:

Step 1: **Look at the digit to the *right* of the place to which you are rounding.**

Step 2: **If the digit is *5 or more*, increase the digit being rounded by 1. If the digit is *less than 5*, leave the digit being rounded the same.**

Step 3: **Change all the digits to the right of the digit being rounded to zeros. If these digits are to the right of a decimal point, simply drop the digits.**

Example

The following place-value table shows 7,152.

Thousands	Hundreds	Tens	Ones
7	1	5	2

7,152 rounded to the nearest **ten** is 7,150.

7,152 rounded to the nearest **hundred** is 7,200.

7,152 rounded to the nearest **thousand** is 7,000.

Example

The following place-value table shows 2.475.

Ones	Decimal Point	Tenths	Hundredths	Thousandths
2	•	4	7	5

2.475 rounded to the nearest **hundredth** is 2.48.

2.475 rounded to the nearest **tenth** is 2.5.

2.475 rounded to the nearest **one** is 2.

Practice

1. What is 2,639.265 rounded to the nearest one? _____

2. What is 5,934.806 rounded to the nearest hundredth? _____

3. Tyler's uncle bought a new truck for $25,655. What was the price of the truck rounded to the nearest $1,000?

_____

4. After her first five tests, Emily's average score was 88.461. What was her average score rounded to the nearest tenth?

_____

Directions: For Numbers 5 through 10, round 8,059.416 to the nearest place value given.

5. hundredth: _____

6. tenth: _____

7. one: _____

8. ten: _____

9. hundred: _____

10. thousand: _____

Rounding fractions and mixed numbers

When rounding fractions and mixed numbers to the nearest $\frac{1}{2}$, it is important to know whether a fraction is less than, equal to, or greater than $\frac{1}{4}$ and $\frac{3}{4}$. If the fraction is $\frac{3}{4}$ **or greater**, drop the fraction and increase the whole number by one. If the fraction is $\frac{1}{4}$ **or greater but less than** $\frac{3}{4}$, change the fraction to $\frac{1}{2}$ and leave the whole number the same. If the fraction is **less than** $\frac{1}{4}$, drop the fraction and leave the whole number the same.

Example

Round the following numbers to the nearest $\frac{1}{2}$.

$$55\frac{2}{9} \qquad \frac{6}{7} \qquad 25\frac{1}{3}$$

$55\frac{2}{9}$ rounded to the nearest $\frac{1}{2}$ is 55.

$\frac{6}{7}$ rounded to the nearest $\frac{1}{2}$ is 1.

$25\frac{1}{3}$ rounded to the nearest $\frac{1}{2}$ is $25\frac{1}{2}$.

Practice

Directions: For Numbers 1 through 6, round the fractions and mixed numbers to the nearest $\frac{1}{2}$.

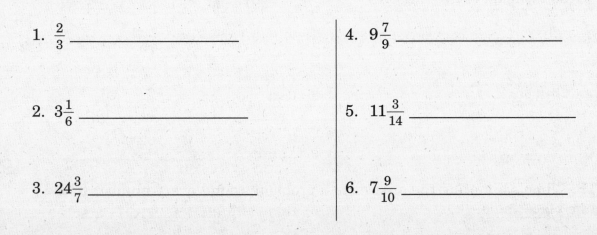

1. $\frac{2}{3}$ _____

2. $3\frac{1}{6}$ _____

3. $24\frac{3}{7}$ _____

4. $9\frac{7}{9}$ _____

5. $11\frac{3}{14}$ _____

6. $7\frac{9}{10}$ _____

Solving problems using estimation and mental math

Sometimes, you might come across a problem in which the calculations are too difficult to do without a calculator. This is where estimation and mental math come in handy. You can round each number and then use mental math to calculate the rounded numbers in your head. This will give you a good estimate of the answer.

Example

A delivery truck is bringing appliances from its warehouse to various stores in northwest Ohio. The truck will stop in Lima, Findlay, Toledo, and Mansfield. The distances traveled will be 88 miles, 33 miles, 45 miles, and 103 miles. About how many miles will this truck travel?

In this example, round each number to the nearest ten.

88 rounds to 90.

33 rounds to 30.

45 rounds to 50.

103 rounds to 100.

Now use mental math to add the rounded numbers together.

90 + 30 + 50 + 100 = 270

The truck will travel about 270 miles altogether.

To find out how close the estimate is to the actual amount, add the original numbers together.

88 + 33 + 45 + 103 = 269

The actual distance the truck will travel is 269 miles. This is very close to the estimate of 270 miles.

TIP: When estimating the answer to a problem, round every number to the same place value.

Practice

Directions: Use rounding to estimate the answers for Numbers 1 through 5. Then calculate the actual answers.

1. The art teacher had a block of clay to use for art projects. She cut it into four pieces and weighed them: $13\frac{3}{8}$ pounds, $12\frac{2}{3}$ pounds, $11\frac{1}{4}$ pounds, and $15\frac{3}{4}$ pounds. How much did the original block of clay weigh?

2. There are 8 sections in the football stadium, each having a seating capacity of 318. How many seats are there in the stadium?

3. Nick wants to estimate the total number of fish in three tanks at the aquarium. A guide tells him that the numbers of fish in each tank are 72, 129, and 36. How many fish are there altogether?

4. Gloria took two friends to lunch. The food orders cost $8.95, $7.83, and $9.14. How much did Gloria spend for the three orders?

5. Cliff walked around the stadium selling bags of peanuts. For a 4-week period, his weekly total sales were 1,011, 892, 757, and 923 bags of peanuts. How many bags of peanuts did Cliff sell altogether?

Problem-Solving Steps

The following example shows the steps you can use to solve real-life problems.

Example

Last year, Mark had 247 stamps in his collection. This year, he bought 98 stamps and then sold 53. He now has 106 more stamps than his friend, Jim. How many stamps does Mark now have?

Step 1: **Take time to study the problem.**

What does the problem want you to figure out?

You need to find the total number of stamps Mark has, because the last sentence asks: "How many stamps does Mark now have?"

Step 2: **Evaluate the information given.**

What information does the problem give?

Mark had 247 stamps last year.

Mark bought 98 stamps and then sold 53 this year.

Mark now has 106 more stamps than his friend, Jim.

Do you have all the information needed to solve the problem?

Yes, there is enough information to solve the problem.

Have you been given extra information that is not needed to solve the problem?

Yes. Mark now has 106 more stamps than his friend, Jim. This information is not needed to solve the problem.

Step 3: **Select the operation(s) needed to solve the problem.**

You need to use these two operations:

addition (since he **bought** stamps)

subtraction (since he **sold** stamps)

Step 4: **Estimate a reasonable answer.**

Round the numbers to the nearest ten.

247 rounds to 250.

98 rounds to 100.

53 rounds to 50.

Add and subtract the rounded numbers to get an estimate.

$250 + 100 - 50 = 300$

The estimated answer is about 300 stamps.

Step 5: **Do the math and check your answer.**

$$247 \quad + \quad 98 \quad = \quad 345 \qquad\qquad 345 \quad - \quad 53 \quad = \quad 292$$

| stamps last year | stamps bought | ⎣———total———⎦ | | stamps sold | stamps Mark has now |

The answer is 292. The estimated answer is 300, so 292 seems reasonable.

Check your answer using the original problem.

$$
\begin{array}{r}
292 \\
+\ 53 \\
\hline
345
\end{array}
\qquad\qquad
\begin{array}{r}
345 \\
-\ 98 \\
\hline
247
\end{array}
$$

Mark now has 292 stamps in his collection.

Problem-Solving Strategies

The following strategies may be helpful when you are solving real-life problems.

- Draw a picture.
- Look for a pattern.
- Guess and check.
- Act it out.
- Make a table.
- Work a simpler problem.
- Work backwards.

Practice

Directions: Use the step-by-step method to solve the following real-life problem.

The following figure shows the dimensions of the construction site for a new house. It is surrounded by a fence that is 10 feet away from and parallel to the walls of the house. The fence is 10 feet tall. Find the total length of fence that was used.

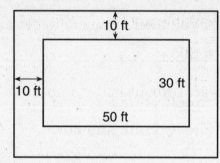

Step 1: **Take time to study the problem.**

    1. What does the problem want you to figure out?

    _____

Step 2: **Evaluate the information given.**

    2. What information does the problem give?

    _____

    _____

    _____

    3. Do you have all the information needed to solve the problem? If not, what information is missing?

    _____

    4. Have you been given extra information that is not needed to solve the problem?

    _____

Step 3: Select the operation(s) needed to solve the problem.

5. What operation or operations will you use to solve the problem?

   _____

Step 4: Estimate a reasonable answer.

6. Estimate a reasonable answer to the problem.

   _____

Step 5: Do the math and check your answer.

7. What is your answer? _____

8. Is it close to your estimate? _____

9. Have you followed all of the necessary steps? _____

10. Is your answer reasonable? _____

Achievement Practice

1. Jason and Sophie each have 6 rolls of film to develop. Each of Jason's rolls has 24 pictures. Each of Sophie's rolls has 36 pictures. How many more pictures will Sophie have developed than Jason?

   A. 12

   B. 72

   C. 144

   D. 216

2. After 85 games in the baseball season, Rich has reached base 39.894% of the times he has batted. What is this percent rounded to the nearest tenth?

   A. 40.0%

   B. 39.9%

   C. 39.8%

   D. 39.0%

3. The following sign at the window shows regular admission prices for the art museum.

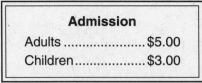

   Admission is half price on Tuesdays. If Kenny spent $35.50 on tickets on Tuesday, which combination of tickets could he have bought?

   A. 5 adults, 4 children

   B. 7 adults, 6 children

   C. 9 adults, 9 children

   D. 10 adults, 7 children

4. When rounding to the nearest $\frac{1}{2}$, which fraction rounds to 18?

    A. $17\frac{13}{15}$

    B. $18\frac{7}{12}$

    C. $17\frac{4}{9}$

    D. $18\frac{2}{3}$

5. Which number is rounded to the nearest one?

    A. 0.355

    B. $10\frac{1}{2}$

    C. 200.05

    D. 1,836

6. What is 12.488 rounded to the nearest tenth?

    A. 12.49

    B. 12.5

    C. 10

    D. 12

7. What is 1,593,025 rounded to the nearest ten thousand?

    A. 1,593,030

    B. 1,593,000

    C. 1,590,000

    D. 1,600,000

8. What is 5,473.125 rounded to the nearest hundredth?

    A. 5,400

    B. 5,470

    C. 5,473.12

    D. 5,473.13

9. When rounding to the nearest one, which number rounds to 322?

    A. 321.15

    B. 321.619

    C. 322.502

    D. 322.8

10. Ben made $809.75 this summer mowing 79 lawns. If he charged the same amount for each lawn, **about** how much did Ben charge per lawn?

    A. $9

    B. $10

    C. $11

    D. $12

11. Chad went on a five-day hiking trip in the mountains. The following table shows the number of miles he hiked each day.

Miles Hiked

Fri.	Sat.	Sun.	Mon.	Tues.
$1\frac{4}{5}$	$4\frac{1}{8}$	$3\frac{7}{10}$	$6\frac{11}{25}$	$2\frac{5}{9}$

In the box below, round each number to the nearest $\frac{1}{2}$. Then add the rounded numbers to estimate the number of miles Chad hiked altogether.

12. Christie bought 4 bracelets and 6 T-shirts. The bracelets cost $6.89 each. All the T-shirts cost the same amount. If Christie spent a total of $114.56 on bracelets and T-shirts, what was the price of each T-shirt?

    A. $12.50

    B. $13.50

    C. $14.50

    D. $15.50

13. Heather rode her bike 8.2 miles on Wednesday, $8\frac{7}{10}$ miles on Thursday, 5.8 miles on Friday, and $10\frac{3}{5}$ miles on Saturday. If you round each number to the nearest $\frac{1}{2}$, **about** how many miles did Heather ride altogether?

    A. 31

    B. 32

    C. 33

    D. 35

14. A hawk is flying 350 feet above a field. It dives 225 feet toward the ground, then turns and flies up 170 feet. How far above the field is the hawk now?

    A. 295 ft

    B. 395 ft

    C. 520 ft

    D. 745 ft

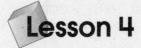
Lesson 4

Ratio, Proportion, and Percent

In this lesson, you will review the relationships between ratios, proportions, and percents. You will also solve problems involving equivalent ratios and rates.

Ratio

A **ratio** compares two numbers. Ratios can be written in one of the following ways.

> 2 to 3   2:3 $\frac{2}{3}$

◢ Example

What is the ratio of stars to moons and the ratio of moons to stars?

There are 5 stars and 3 moons. The ratio of stars to moons can be written as 5 to 3, 5:3, or $\frac{5}{3}$. The ratio of moons to stars can be written as 3 to 5, 3:5, or $\frac{3}{5}$.

◢ Example

What is the ratio of footballs to baseballs?

There are 4 footballs and 8 baseballs. The ratio of footballs to baseballs can be written as 4 to 8, 4:8, or $\frac{4}{8}$. The ratio can also be written in lowest terms as 1 to 2, 1:2, or $\frac{1}{2}$.

 **Practice**

Directions: In 1879, Thomas Edison, from Milan, Ohio, invented the light bulb.
Use the following drawing to answer Numbers 1 through 3.

1. What is the ratio of shaded bulbs to the total number of bulbs? _____

2. What is the ratio of unshaded bulbs to the total number of bulbs? _____

3. What is the ratio of shaded bulbs to unshaded bulbs? _____

Directions: Use the following drawing to answer Numbers 4 and 5.

4. What is the ratio of pears to apples? _____

5. What is the ratio of apples to pears? _____

6. What is the ratio of shaded keys to unshaded keys, in lowest terms?

_____

7. What is the ratio of doors to windows in your classroom? _____

Proportion

A **proportion** states that two ratios are equal.

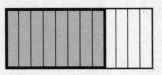 **Example**

The drawing on the left shows that $\frac{8}{12}$ of the figure is shaded. The drawing on the right shows that $\frac{2}{3}$ of the figure is shaded.

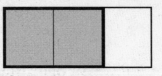

You can see from the drawings that the ratios $\frac{8}{12}$ and $\frac{2}{3}$ are equivalent. Therefore, the following proportion can be written.

$$\frac{8}{12} = \frac{2}{3}$$

The **cross products** of a proportion are equal. Multiply the numbers that are diagonally across from each other to get the cross products.

$$\frac{8}{12} \diagdown\kern-1.2em\diagup \frac{2}{3}$$

$$8 \cdot 3 = 12 \cdot 2$$

$$24 = 24$$

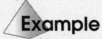 **Example**

The ratios $\frac{4}{7}$ and $\frac{52}{91}$ are equal. Use cross products to show that the proportion is true.

$$\frac{4}{7} = \frac{52}{91}$$

$$4 \cdot 91 = 7 \cdot 52$$

$$364 = 364$$

A proportion can be used to find the missing value in a problem-solving situation. A **variable** is a letter that can be used to represent the missing value.

Example

Pencils are on sale, 3 for 36¢. How much money does Elysa need to buy 6 pencils?

Step 1: **Set up a proportion.**

$$\text{pencils} \rightarrow \frac{3}{36} = \frac{6}{x} \leftarrow \text{pencils} \atop \leftarrow \text{money}$$

Step 2: **Multiply to get cross products.**

$$3 \cdot x = 36 \cdot 6$$
$$3 \cdot x = 216$$

Step 3: **Simplify the equation.** Divide both sides of the equation by 3 so that x is by itself on one side of the equation.

$$\frac{3 \cdot x}{3} = \frac{216}{3}$$
$$x = 72$$

Step 4: **Check to see that the cross products are equal by substituting your answer for the unknown number.**

$$\frac{3}{36} = \frac{6}{72}$$

$$3 \cdot 72 = 36 \cdot 6$$

$$216 = 216$$

Elysa needs 72¢ to buy 6 pencils.

Practice

Directions: For Numbers 1 through 6, determine whether the proportion is true or false. Write your answer on the line.

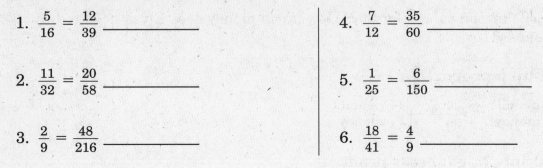

1. $\frac{5}{16} = \frac{12}{39}$ _____

2. $\frac{11}{32} = \frac{20}{58}$ _____

3. $\frac{2}{9} = \frac{48}{216}$ _____

4. $\frac{7}{12} = \frac{35}{60}$ _____

5. $\frac{1}{25} = \frac{6}{150}$ _____

6. $\frac{18}{41} = \frac{4}{9}$ _____

Directions: For Numbers 7 and 8, solve each proportion.

7. $\frac{3}{6} = \frac{x}{8}$ _____

8. $\frac{5}{9} = \frac{10}{x}$ _____

9. Maria can read 15 pages in 20 minutes. At this rate, how long will it take Maria to read 180 pages?

_____

10. Jim walks at an average rate of 4 miles per hour. At this rate, how long will it take Jim to walk 10 miles?

_____

11. Which proportion is true?

   A. $\frac{3}{4} = \frac{5}{6}$

   B. $\frac{2}{5} = \frac{9}{23}$

   C. $\frac{5}{8} = \frac{35}{56}$

   D. $\frac{9}{10} = \frac{99}{100}$

12. Which proportion is false?

   A. $\frac{10}{12} = \frac{15}{18}$

   B. $\frac{15}{20} = \frac{23}{30}$

   C. $\frac{7}{15} = \frac{21}{45}$

   D. $\frac{9}{25} = \frac{36}{100}$

Proportion and Percent

When you want to find a missing percent, set up a proportion, cross multiply, and then solve. Your proportion can be set up the following way.

$$\frac{part}{whole} = \frac{x}{100}$$

Example

What percent of 16 is 4?

$$\frac{4}{16} = \frac{x}{100} \qquad \text{(Set up a proportion.)}$$

$$16 \cdot x = 400 \qquad \text{(Cross multiply.)}$$

$$x = 25 \qquad \text{(Divide both sides by 16.)}$$

4 is 25% of 16.

Practice

1. What is 40% of 30? _____

2. 123 is what percent of 150? _____

3. What percent of 1,000 is 5? _____

4. 98 is what percent of 112? _____

5. The Nevin family tipped their waitress $19 for a $95 dinner bill. What percent of the dinner bill did the Nevin family leave for the tip?

_____

6. Duke earned $250 washing cars last summer. He spent all of his earnings on a new stereo and a new jacket. If Duke paid $190 for the stereo, what percent of his summer earnings did he spend on the jacket?

_____

Percent of Increase and Decrease

The percent of increase or decrease is found by using a ratio. You need to convert the ratio into a decimal, and then into a percent.

To find the **percent of increase**, use the following ratio.

$$\frac{\text{new amount} - \text{original amount}}{\text{original amount}}$$

 **Example**

Jude's allowance went from $5.25 per week to $6.25 per week. What is the percent of increase? Round to the nearest percent.

$$\frac{\text{new amount} - \text{original amount}}{\text{original amount}} = \frac{6.25 - 5.25}{5.25}$$

$$= \frac{1}{5.25}$$

$$= 0.19047619\ldots$$

Jude's allowance increased by about 19%.

To find the **percent of decrease**, use the following ratio.

$$\frac{\text{original amount} - \text{new amount}}{\text{original amount}}$$

Example

A compact disc that costs $15.95 drops in price to $11.99. What is the percent of decrease? Round to the nearest percent.

$$\frac{\text{original amount} - \text{new amount}}{\text{original amount}} = \frac{15.95 - 11.99}{15.95}$$

$$= \frac{3.96}{15.95}$$

$$= 0.248275862\ldots$$

The price of the compact disc decreased by about 25%.

Practice

Directions: For Numbers 1 through 7, round the percent of increase or decrease to the nearest percent.

1. Shane bought a new car for $23,500. Two years later, the car's value was $16,360. What is the percent of decrease?

   _____

2. Lucy's cell phone bill went from $37.93 in June to $26.70 in July. What is the percent of decrease?

   _____

3. Jake's bowling average went from 145 to 172. What is the percent of increase?

   _____

4. In the past five years, the price of a milk shake at Sloopy's Shake Shop went from $1.69 to $1.99. What is the percent of increase?

   _____

5. Michael's time in the 400-meter dash went from 71 seconds to 62 seconds. What is the percent of decrease?

   _____

6. The cost for a child's movie ticket went from $4.50 to $4.75. What is the percent of increase?

   _____

7. Keith bought a new tent that had a sale price of $20.74. The original price of the tent was $82.99. What is the percent of decrease?

   _____

Achievement Practice

1. Which proportion is true?

    A. $\frac{8}{9} = \frac{64}{81}$

    B. $\frac{3}{8} = \frac{27}{72}$

    C. $\frac{12}{13} = \frac{25}{26}$

    D. $\frac{1}{5} = \frac{7}{34}$

2. Simone earned $5.55 for selling 3 baskets of apples. How much can Simone earn for selling 7 baskets?

    A. $38.85

    B. $16.65

    C. $12.95

    D. $11.00

3. Which proportion is true?

    A. $\frac{2}{3} = \frac{15}{20}$

    B. $\frac{3}{4} = \frac{12}{18}$

    C. $\frac{4}{5} = \frac{22}{25}$

    D. $\frac{5}{6} = \frac{20}{24}$

4. What is the ratio of unshaded stars to shaded stars in the following picture?

    A. $\frac{2}{5}$

    B. $\frac{2}{7}$

    C. $\frac{5}{7}$

    D. $\frac{7}{21}$

5. What is the ratio of shaded circles to unshaded circles in the following picture?

    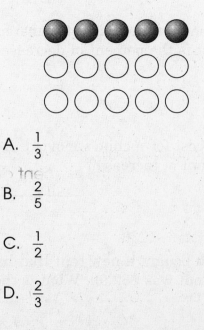

    A. $\frac{1}{3}$

    B. $\frac{2}{5}$

    C. $\frac{1}{2}$

    D. $\frac{2}{3}$

6. Rusty is building a doghouse for his dog, Wheezer. He is making the dimensions of the doghouse proportional to his own house, which has a length of 54 feet and a width of 36 feet. If Wheezer's new home is going to have a length of 6 feet, what will be the width?

    A.   4 feet

    B.   7 feet

    C.   9 feet

    D. 12 feet

7. Johnny ran the first 3.2 km of a 10-km race in 16 minutes. If he keeps the same pace throughout the race, how long will it take Johnny to run the entire race?

    A. 40 minutes

    B. 46 minutes

    C. 50 minutes

    D. 64 minutes

8. There are 20 computers at the school library and 80 sixth-grade students. What is the ratio of computers to sixth-grade students?

    A. 1 to 2

    B. 1 to 4

    C. 3 to 4

    D. 6 to 9

9. Jen found a pair of volleyball shoes that were marked down from $64.99 to $49.99. What is the percent of decrease?

    A. about 20%

    B. about 23%

    C. about 27%

    D. about 30%

10. What is the ratio of shaded squares to the total number of squares in the following grid?

    A. 77:23

    B. 23:77

    C. 23:100

    D. 77:100

11. Tamara's calendar sales went from $230 last year to $575. What is the percent of increase?

    A. 150%

    B. 140%

    C. 130%

    D. 120%

12. In the box below, use a proportion to find 15% of 240. Show your work.

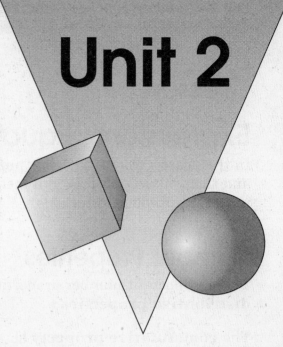

Unit 2

Patterns, Functions, and Algebra

People all around you in your everyday life are using patterns, functions, and algebra. For example, an Olympic diver's score is equal to the scores from the judges multiplied by the dive's degree of difficulty. Bank officers, architects, toy makers, auto mechanics, engineers, salespeople, and many others use patterns and equations to figure out solutions to all kinds of problems.

In this unit, you will evaluate algebraic expressions and solve linear equations and inequalities. You will identify relationships between two variables by writing equations, creating tables of ordered pairs, and graphing your results. Finally, you will analyze, determine rules for, and extend a variety of patterns.

In This Unit

Expressions, Equations, and Inequalities

Graphing Equations and Inequalities

Patterns and Functions

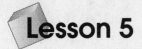

Lesson 5

Expressions, Equations, and Inequalities

In this lesson, you will review number properties. You will evaluate expressions and then solve equations and inequalities. Finally, you will write equations to represent problem situations.

Number Properties

Three important number properties are the **commutative**, **associative**, and **distributive properties**.

The **commutative property** shows that the **order** of the numbers does not change the sum of an addition problem or the product of a multiplication problem.

Commutative Property	
Addition	**Multiplication**
$a + b = b + a$	$a \bullet b = b \bullet a$
$15 + 9 = 9 + 15$	$3 \bullet 9 = 9 \bullet 3$
$24 = 24$	$27 = 27$

The **associative property** shows that the **grouping** of the numbers does not change the sum or the product.

Associative Property	
Addition	**Multiplication**
$(a + b) + c = a + (b + c)$	$(a \bullet b) \bullet c = a \bullet (b \bullet c)$
$(11 + 6) + 8 = 11 + (6 + 8)$	$(4 \bullet 5) \bullet 3 = 4 \bullet (5 \bullet 3)$
$17 + 8 = 11 + 14$	$20 \bullet 3 = 4 \bullet 15$
$25 = 25$	$60 = 60$

The **distributive property** uses both addition and multiplication.

Distributive Property
$a(b + c) = a(b) + a(c)$
$2(1 + 4) = 2(1) + 2(4)$
$2(5) = 2 + 8$
$10 = 10$

Practice

Directions: For Numbers 1 through 7, write the property that is represented by the given equation.

1. $6 \cdot 11 = 11 \cdot 6$ _____

2. $2(x + 3) = 2x + 6$ _____

3. $13 + 22 = 22 + 13$ _____

4. $h \cdot 5 = 5 \cdot h$ _____

5. $(14 \cdot 3) \cdot 8 = 14 \cdot (3 \cdot 8)$ _____

6. $3(6 + 2) = 3(6) + 3(2)$ _____

7. $(x + y) + z = x + (y + z)$ _____

8. What properties are used in the following equation?

   $8(11 + 6) = 11(8) + 6(8)$

   A. commutative only

   B. associative and distributive

   C. associative and commutative

   D. commutative and distributive

9. For which operation(s) is the commutative property true?

   A. addition only

   B. subtraction and division

   C. addition and subtraction

   D. multiplication and addition

Evaluating Expressions

An **expression** is a mathematical phrase made up of variables, symbols, and/or numbers and operations. To evaluate an expression with one or more variables or symbols, substitute the given number(s) for the variable(s) or symbol(s). Then follow the order of operations to simplify the expression.

 **Example**

Evaluate $n + 24$ for $n = 18$.

Given that $n = 18$, substitute 18 for n in the expression and simplify.

$n + 24$

$18 + 24$ (Substitute 18 for n.)

    42   (Add.)

The answer is 42.

Example

Evaluate $2x + 13$ for $x = 25$.

Given that $x = 25$, substitute 25 for x in the expression and simplify.

$2x + 13$

$2(25) + 13$ (Substitute 25 for x.)

$50 + 13$ (Multiply 2 and 25.)

    63   (Add.)

The answer is 63.

Practice

Directions: For Numbers 1 through 7, evaluate each expression for $y = 3$ and $z = -6$.

1. $15 + z$

2. $4 - (z + 10)$

3. $11 + y \cdot 3$

4. $30 + z$

5. $y \cdot 17$

6. $(z - 18) \div 4$

7. $y \div 3 + z = ?$

   A. -5

   B. 1

   C. 7

   D. 8

Directions: For Numbers 8 through 14, evaluate each expression for $a = 5$, $b = -2$, and $c = 4$.

8. $4c \div 8$

9. $25 + a$

10. $3a - 19$

11. $(b - 9) \cdot 5$

12. $13c + 23$

13. $100 \div (b - 3)$

14. $2a + 20 = ?$

    A. 10

    B. 15

    C. 25

    D. 30

Solving Equations and Inequalities

An **equation** is a mathematical sentence showing two expressions that are equal. An **inequality** is a mathematical sentence showing two expressions that are not equal. To solve an equation or inequality, you need to get the variable alone on one side of the equation using inverse (opposite) operations. Remember, when you multiply or divide both sides of an inequality by a negative number, you need to flip the inequality sign.

 **Example**

Solve the following equation for m.

$7 + m = 30$

Use inverse operations to get the variable alone on one side of the equation.

$$7 + m = 30$$
$$7 + m - \mathbf{7} = 30 - \mathbf{7} \qquad \text{(Subtract 7 from both sides.)}$$
$$m = 23$$

The answer is $m = 23$.

 **Example**

Solve the following equation for d.

$-12 \cdot d < 84$

Use inverse operations to get the variable alone on one side of the inequality.

$$-12 \cdot d < 84$$

$$\frac{-12 \cdot d}{-12} > \frac{84}{-12} \qquad \text{(Divide both sides by } -12. \text{ Switch the sign.)}$$

$$d > -7$$

The answer is $d > -7$.

Practice

Directions: For Numbers 1 through 12, solve each equation or inequality for the given variable.

1. $25 + g = 75$

2. $n - 20 > 40$

3. $-7y = 210$

4. $s \div 5 \leq 12$

5. $31 + m > -85$

6. $-32 + r = 41$

   A. $r = -9$
   B. $r = 13$
   C. $r = 59$
   D. $r = 73$

7. $p \div 4 = 53$

8. $h \cdot 8 < 112$

9. $12 - t = -15$

10. $-11x \leq 110$

11. $\frac{k}{5} = -15$

12. $d - 16 \geq 84$

    A. $d \geq 100$
    B. $d \geq 58$
    C. $d \geq -58$
    D. $d \geq -100$

Writing Equations

A variable can be used to represent a missing number in an equation. You can write equations to represent different problem situations.

▲ Example

The annual Popcorn Festival in Marion County is the second-largest festival in the United States. At one snack stand, there were 217 bags of colored popcorn. 122 bags had blue popcorn; the rest had red popcorn. How many bags of red popcorn were at the snack stand?

First, find all the information you need to know.

122 = bags of blue popcorn

r = bags of red popcorn

217 = total number of bags of popcorn

Now you can write an equation.

blue popcorn → $122 + r = 217$ ← **total number of bags of popcorn**

↑
red popcorn

The following equation can be used to represent the problem situation.

$$122 + r = 217$$

There may be more than one way to write an equation to represent the problem situation. The following equations can also be written.

$$r + 122 = 217 \qquad 217 - r = 122 \qquad 217 - 122 = r$$

Practice

Directions: For Numbers 1 through 5, write an equation that represents each problem situation.

1. Megan bought 180 eggs. How many dozens of eggs did she buy?

2. Walter laid two stone paths. Their total distance was 69 feet. One path was 7 feet longer than the other. How long was each path?

3. Gina bought two packages of beads for making bracelets. One package had 4 times as many beads as the other package. She bought 225 beads altogether. How many beads were in the smaller packet?

4. The automatic tennis server holds 110 tennis balls that shoot out one at a time. Andre's 3 friends took turns hitting 27 balls each. Andre hit the remaining balls. How many tennis balls did Andre hit?

5. Angela did 5 fewer than twice as many sit-ups as Paula. Between the two of them, they did a total of 136 sit-ups. How many sit-ups did Angela do?

Achievement Practice

1. Evaluate the following expression for $y = 6$.

    $25 + 2y$

    A. 31
    B. 33
    C. 35
    D. 37

2. Which equation shows the commutative property?

    A. $2x = 2x$
    B. $2x + 3 = 3 + 2x$
    C. $2x - 3 = 2(x - 3)$
    D. $2(x + 3) = 2x + 6$

3. Solve the following equation for q.

    $q + 25 = 84$

    A. $q = 59$
    B. $q = 60$
    C. $q = 95$
    D. $q = 109$

4. Catherine spent a total of 6 hours at the school gymnasium for the middle-school dance. If the dance lasted 2.5 hours, which equation can be used to find h, the number of hours Catherine spent decorating and cleaning up the gym?

    A. $2.5 + h = 6$
    B. $6 + 2.5 = h$
    C. $h - 6 = 2.5$
    D. $2.5 + h + 2.5 = 6$

5. Evaluate the following expression for $x = 2$, $y = 3$, and $z = -4$.

    $-4xy - 2z + 3$

    A. 35

    B. 19

    C. −13

    D. −29

6. While driving through Knox County, Ohio, Alex counted a total of 36 deer in 9 different fields. Which equation can be used to find d, the average number of deer seen in each field?

    A. $9 + d = 36$

    B. $d \div 36 = 9$

    C. $36d = 9$

    D. $9d = 36$

7. How can the following expression be written using the distributive property?

    $8(5 + 12)$

    A. $8 \cdot 5 \cdot 12$

    B. $(8 \cdot 5) + 12$

    C. $(8 \cdot 5) + (5 \cdot 12)$

    D. $(8 \cdot 5) + (8 \cdot 12)$

8. In the box below, solve the following inequality for x. Show your work.

    $4x + 10 < 50$

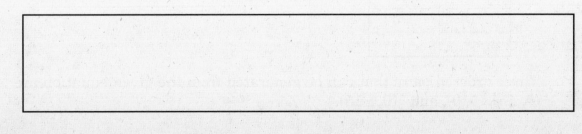

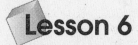 **Lesson 6**

Graphing Equations and Inequalities

In this lesson, you will graph linear equations and inequalities. You will also graph equations from real-world situations and compare the rates of change between two different equations.

Generating Ordered Pairs

Some equations contain two different variables, usually x and y. An equation can be used to find the relationship between x and y. You can find a set of **ordered pairs** (x, y) that satisfies any given equation. An equation can be stated either verbally or algebraically. Here's an example:

Verbally: Fifteen minus the product of three and a number, x, is equal to another number, y.

Algebraically: $15 - 3x = y$

▸ **Example**

Find three ordered pairs that can be generated from the following equation.

$$15 - 3x = y$$

Substitute any value into the equation for either x or y, and then solve for the other variable.

$x = 0$	$y = 0$	$x = 10$
$15 - 3(0) = y$	$15 - 3x = 0$	$15 - 3(10) = y$
$15 - 0 = y$	$-3x = -15$	$15 - 30 = y$
$15 = y$	$x = 5$	$-15 = y$

These values can also be put into a table.

x	y
0	15
5	0
10	-15

Three ordered pairs that can be generated from the given equation are $(0, 15)$, $(5, 0)$, and $(10, -15)$.

Practice

Directions: For Numbers 1 through 5, find five ordered pairs that can be generated from each verbal or algebraic equation.

1. $4x - 10 = y$

    ordered pairs: _____

2. A number, x, divided by two-fifths is equal to another number, y.

    ordered pairs: _____

3. $5 + \frac{1}{3}x = y$

    ordered pairs: _____

4. Twenty-five less than the product of a number, x, and five is equal to another number, y.

    ordered pairs: _____

5. $\dfrac{x + 7}{2} = y$

x	y

Graphing Linear Equations

To graph a linear equation, find a set of ordered pairs that when substituted into the equation makes the equation true. Use a table of values to generate at least three ordered pairs by choosing any value for either x or y. Then graph the ordered pairs and draw a line through them to show the solutions to the equation.

Example

Graph the equation $3x + y = 6$.

Substitute $x = 0$, $y = 0$, and $x = 4$ into the equation to find three ordered pairs. List the values in a table.

x	y
0	6
2	0
4	−6

Now plot the three ordered pairs on the coordinate plane. Then draw a line through the points to show all the solutions to the equation.

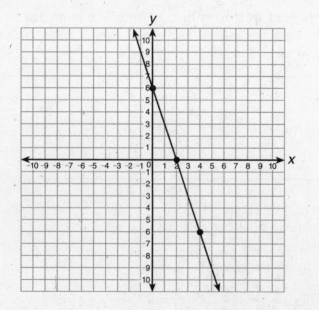

The ordered pairs $(0, 6)$, $(2, 0)$, and $(4, −6)$ are only three solutions to the equation $3x + y = 6$. There are an infinite number of solutions that can be represented by the ordered pairs for every point on the line.

Practice

Directions: For Numbers 1 through 4, fill in the table with three ordered pairs that are solutions to the equation. Then graph the equation.

1. $x - 2y = 8$

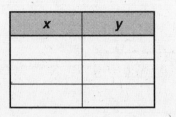

x	y

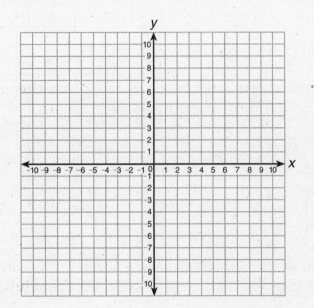

2. $3x + 5y = 15$

x	y

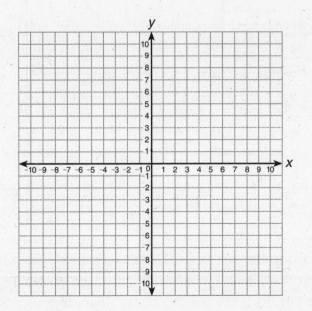

3. $x + y = -7$

x	y

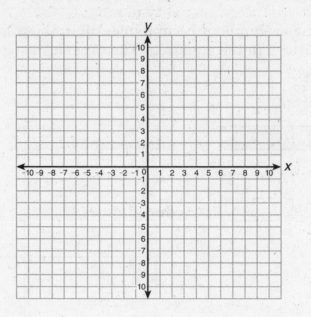

4. $-4x - y = 4$

x	y

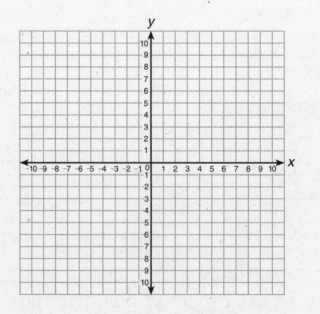

Graphing Linear Inequalities

You can graph a linear inequality in much the same way that you graph a linear equation. However, the graph of a linear inequality includes a shaded region.

◢ Example

Graph the inequality $x + y < -5$.

Step 1: **Replace the inequality symbol with an equal sign.**

$x + y = -5$

Step 2: **Make a table of ordered pairs that are solutions to the equation of the boundary line.**

x	y
-5	0
0	-5
3	-8

Step 3: **Use the ordered pairs to plot and connect the points to form a line.**

If the inequality has a ≥ or ≤ sign, the boundary line should be solid. This indicates that the points on the line **are** part of the solution. If the inequality has a > or < sign, the boundary line should be dashed. This indicates that the points on the line **are not** part of the solution.

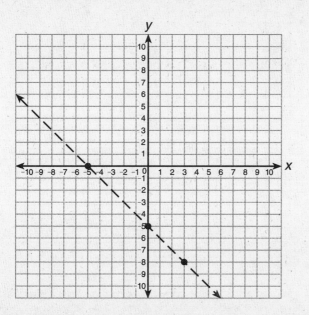

Step 4: **Select and check a test point not on the line.**

A **test point** is any ordered pair that is not on the boundary line.

(0, 0) is always a good choice for a test point if it is not on the boundary line.

Substitute the coordinates of the test point for x and y in the inequality.

$x + y < -5$

$0 + 0 < -5$

$0 < -5$ False

Since 0 is not less than -5, the test point (0, 0) makes the inequality false.

Step 5: **Shade the correct side of the boundary line.**

If the test point makes the inequality **true**, shade the side of the boundary line where the test point is located.

If the test point makes the inequality **false**, shade the side of the boundary line opposite the test point.

In this example, the shading is on the opposite side of the boundary line where (0, 0) is located. Any point in the shaded region is a solution to the inequality.

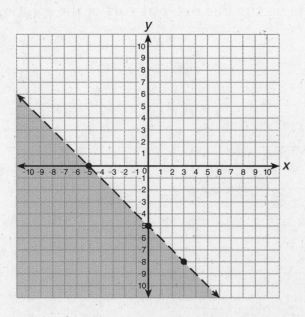

Practice

Directions: For Numbers 1 through 4, fill in the table with three ordered pairs that lie on the boundary line of the inequality. Then graph the inequality.

1. $x - y < 3$

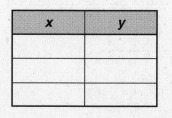

x	y

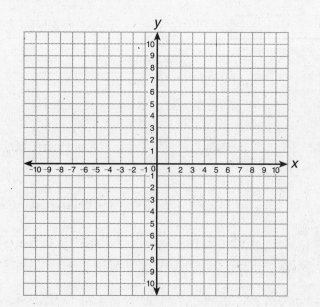

2. $x + y \geq -4$

x	y

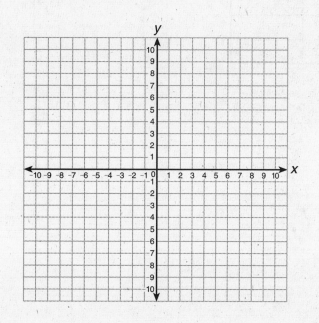

3. $x + 2y \leq 2$

x	y

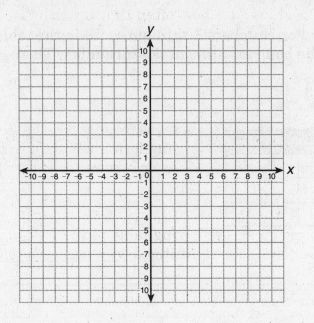

4. $3x - y > -6$

x	y

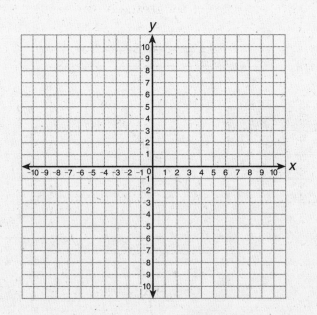

Real-World Situations

Some people don't realize how often they actually use algebra in their lives. There are many algebraic relationships in the real world that you probably don't think about. You can use tables and graphs to represent these situations.

Example

Tina wants to buy some souvenirs while she is on vacation. The sales tax rate is 5%. The following formula is used to find the amount of sales tax, t, that is paid for goods or services that have a cost of c.

$$t = 0.05c$$

Tina made the following table to show the amount of sales tax she would have to pay for eight items with different costs.

Cost (*c*)	$1.00	$2.00	$3.00	$4.00	$5.00	$6.00	$7.00	$8.00
Sales Tax (*t*)	$0.05	$0.10	$0.15	$0.20	$0.25	$0.30	$0.35	$0.40

The ordered pairs from the table were plotted on the following graph. A line was then drawn through the points to represent the amount of sales tax Tina has to pay for items of different cost.

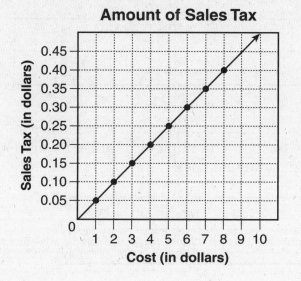

The graph shows that if Tina buys a souvenir for $9.00, she will have to pay $0.45 for sales tax.

Practice

1. The Kelvin temperature scale is sometimes used in science. The relationship between degrees Kelvin, k, and degrees Celsius, c, is represented by the following formula.

   $$k = 273 + c$$

   Make a table of values to show the Kelvin temperatures for the Celsius temperatures of 0°, 15°, 30°, 45°, 60°, 75°, and 90°.

Degrees Celsius (C)							
Degrees Kelvin (K)							

2. Madeline is going to make matching necklaces for her friends. She will need 32 beads for each necklace. The following formula can be used to determine the number of beads, b, she will need for n necklaces.

   $$b = 32n$$

   Make a table of values to show how many beads Madeline will need for 1, 2, 3, 4, 5, 6, and 7 necklaces.

Necklaces (n)							
Beads (b)							

3. Paco made the following table to show the number of miles he drives his truck and the number of gallons of gasoline he uses.

Miles (m)	42	98	140	210	308
Gallons (g)	3	7	10	15	22

   What formula can be used to show the relationship between m, the number of miles driven and g, the number of gallons of gasoline used?

   _____

4. Plot the ordered pairs from the table on the graph. Then draw a line through the points to show the cost of different numbers of tickets.

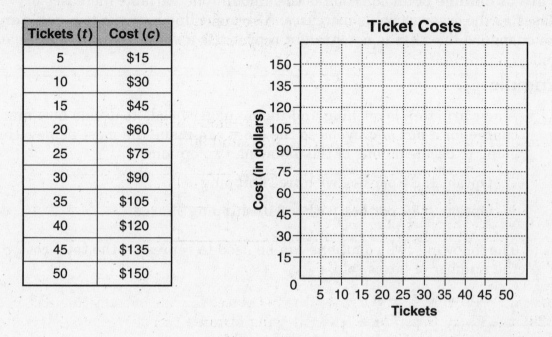

Tickets (*t*)	Cost (*c*)
5	$15
10	$30
15	$45
20	$60
25	$75
30	$90
35	$105
40	$120
45	$135
50	$150

Ticket Costs

5. Plot the ordered pairs from the table on the graph. Then draw a line through the points to show the number of leaves on a plant at the end of each month.

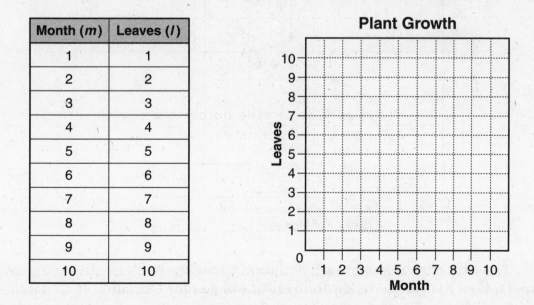

Month (*m*)	Leaves (*l*)
1	1
2	2
3	3
4	4
5	5
6	6
7	7
8	8
9	9
10	10

Plant Growth

Rate of Change

The **rate of change** of an equation is the amount one variable increases or decreases as the other variable increases. A straight line represents a **constant** rate of change. A line that is not straight represents a **variable** rate of change.

Example

A new art store is opening and the manager needs to decide how much to charge for a box of crayons so the store can make the most money. He is going to decide on one of the following two options.

Option 1: $4 per box with free shipping

Option 2: $2 per box with a $10 shipping charge

The following two equations can be used to represent the total cost, c, for the number of boxes sold, b.

Option 1: $c = 4b$

Option 2: $c = 2b + 10$

The following graph represents the two different options.

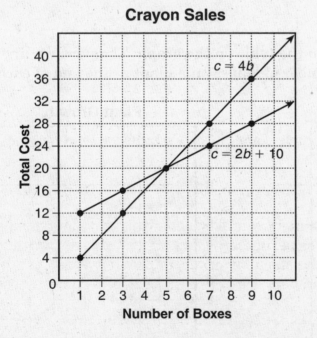

The rate of change for each equation is constant. The rate of change for Option 1 is greater than the rate of change for Option 2. If a customer buys fewer than 5 boxes, Option 2 is a better choice for the store. If a customer buys exactly 5 boxes, both options are the same. If a customer buys more than 5 boxes, Option 1 is a better choice.

Practice

Directions: Use the following information to answer Numbers 1 through 3.

The equation used to find the perimeter of a square, P, is $P = 4s$, where s is the length of a side. The equation used to find the area of a square, A, is $A = s^2$.

1. Graph each equation to represent the perimeter and area of a square as the side length increases.

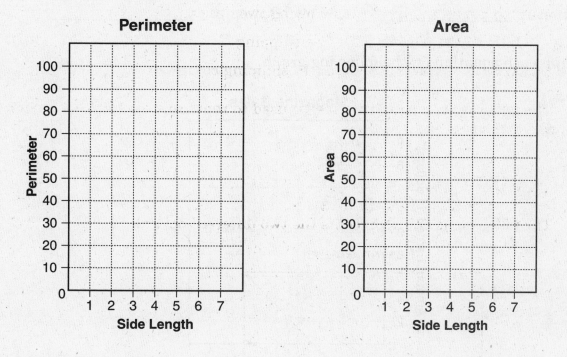

2. Do the perimeter and area have constant or variable rates of change?

   perimeter: _____   area: _____

3. Compare the graphs for perimeter and area. At which side lengths are the graphed numbers greater for perimeter than for area? At which side lengths are the graphed numbers the same for perimeter and for area? At which side lengths are the graphed numbers greater for area than for perimeter?

   _____

   _____

   _____

   _____

Directions: Use the following information to answer Numbers 4 through 7.

Ty is helping his mom sell magazines. He has two options for how she will pay him.

   Option 1: $1 plus $0.50 per magazine

   Option 2: $5 plus $0.25 per magazine

4. Write two equations to represent the amount Ty will earn, a, for each magazine he sells, m.

   Option 1: _____   Option 2: _____

5. Graph each equation on the following graph.

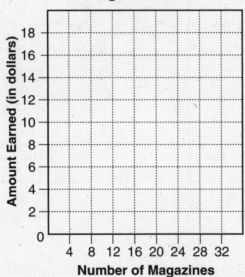

Magazine Sales

6. Do Options 1 and 2 have constant or variable rates of change?

   Option 1: _____   Option 2: _____

7. Based on the number of magazines he sells, explain which option Ty should choose to receive the most money.

   _____

   _____

   _____

Achievement Practice

1. Which set of ordered pairs can be generated from the following equation?

$$y = 2x$$

A. (0, 0), (4, 8), (8, 16)

B. (3, 5), (5, 9), (7, 13)

C. (1, 2), (6, 12), (9, 20)

D. (2, 4), (6, 10), (10, 15)

2. Which equation is shown on the following graph?

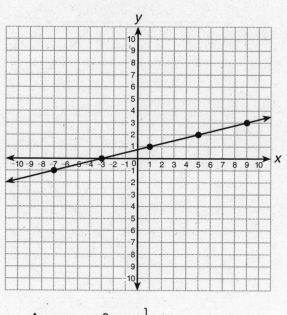

A. $y = -3x + \frac{1}{4}$

B. $y = 4x - \frac{3}{4}$

C. $y = \frac{1}{2}x - 3$

D. $y = \frac{1}{4}x + \frac{3}{4}$

3. Which table of ordered pairs can be generated from the following equation?

$$y = 2x - 9$$

A.

x	y
-3	3
-2	5
-1	7
0	9
1	11

B.

x	y
-1	-11
0	-9
1	-7
2	-5
3	-3

C.

x	y
2	-5
3	-3
4	-1
5	0
6	1

D.

x	y
0	-9
1	-5
2	-1
3	3
4	7

93

4. Which graph shows the solution to the inequality $y \geq -3x + 6$?

5. Which graph shows the solution to the equation $y = x - 5$?

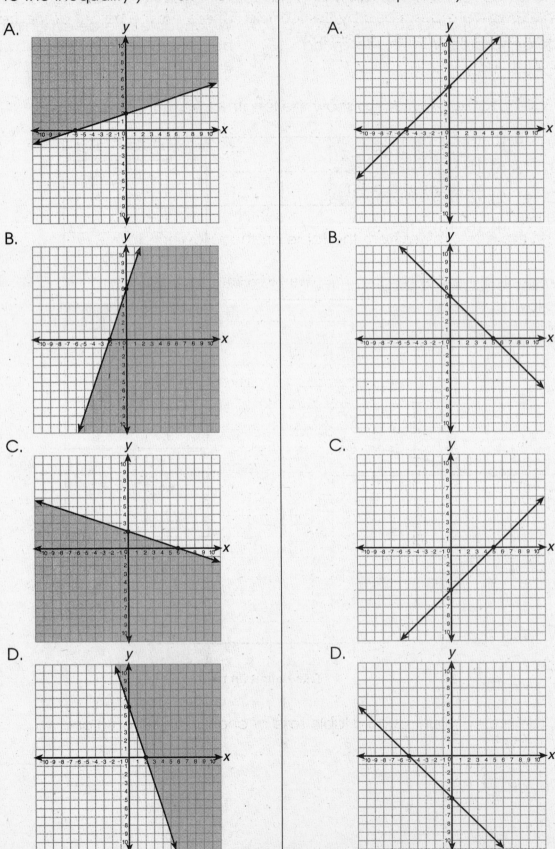

A.

B.

C.

D.

A.

B.

C.

D.

6. Tom planted five trees whose heights were 2 ft, 5 ft, 6 ft, 8 ft, and 10 ft. In the late afternoon, the sun cast a shadow of each tree. The lengths of the shadows were described by this formula, where h is the height of the tree and s is the length of the shadow.

$$s = 1.5h$$

Make a table of values to show the length of each tree's shadow.

Tree Height (h)					
Shadow Length (s)					

Plot the data values from the table on the following graph.

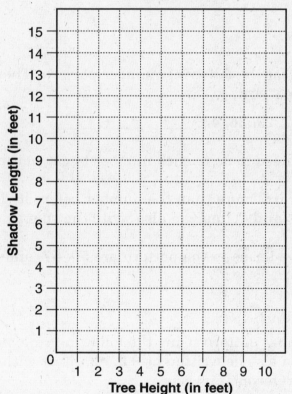

Tree Shadows

Is there a constant or a variable rate of change between h and s?

_____

Lesson 7

Patterns and Functions

In this lesson, you will analyze, describe, extend, and write rules for a variety of patterns. You will also write equations to analyze functions.

Number Patterns

When working with a given set of numbers, you may be asked to find the rule for the pattern that the numbers follow. You can use the rule to find more terms in the number pattern. Sometimes you may be given a rule and asked to create your own number pattern using that rule. These rules may involve one operation or a combination of operations.

Example

Find the rule for the following number pattern. Then find the next three terms in the pattern.

1, 8, 15, 22, 29, 36, 43, _____, _____, _____

What do you need to do to each number to get to the next number?

Each number is 7 more than the number before it. Therefore, the rule for the pattern is **add 7**. You can also write the rule as **+7**.

The next three terms in the pattern are **50**, **57**, and **64**.

Example

Create a number pattern using the following rule: **add 3 then multiply by 2**. This can also be written as **+3, •2**. Start with the number 1 and list the first seven terms.

Start with 1. Add 3 to get the second number. Then multiply the second number by 2 to get the third number. Keep doing this until you have the first seven terms in the pattern. Here is the pattern:

1, 4, 8, 11, 22, 25, 50

Arithmetic sequences

An **arithmetic sequence** is an addition or subtraction number pattern in which the **difference** between any two consecutive terms is constant. This is called the **common difference**. You can use the common difference to find the nth term in a sequence.

 **Example**

What is the 10th term in the following sequence?

4, 10, 16, 22, 28, . . .

This is an arithmetic sequence with a common difference of 6. Use the common difference to extend the sequence to ten terms.

4, 10, 16, 22, 28, 34, 40, 46, 52, 58

The 10th term in the sequence is 58.

Geometric sequences

A **geometric sequence** is a multiplication or division number pattern in which the **ratio** of any two consecutive terms is constant. This ratio is called the **common ratio**. You can use the common ratio to find the nth term in a sequence.

 **Example**

What is the 8th term in the following sequence?

1, 3, 9, 27, . . .

This is a geometric sequence with a common ratio of 3. Use the common ratio to extend the sequence to eight terms.

1, 3, 9, 27, 81, 243, 729, 2,187

The 8th term in the sequence is 2,187.

Number patterns in tables

Number patterns can also be shown in a two-column table. You may see a pattern within the first column, within the second column, or between the first and second columns. Sometimes, you will see all three patterns in one table.

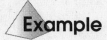**Example**

Find the rule for the pattern in the following table.

x	y
2	4
3	6
4	8
5	10
6	12

The rule for the pattern in column *x* is **add 1 (+1)**. The rule for the pattern in column *y* is **add 2 (+2)**. The rule for the pattern going from a number in column *x* to a number in column *y* is **multiply by 2 (•2)**.

Practice

1. Find the rule for this pattern. Then fill in the next three terms of the pattern.

    40, 35, 30, 25, 20, _____, _____, _____

    rule: _____

2. Find the rule for this pattern. Then fill in the next three terms of the pattern.

    12, 13, 15, 18, 22, __27__, __33__, __40__

    rule: _____

3. Write a number pattern using the rule +10, −5. Start with the number 1 and list seven terms.

    _____

4. What is the 12th term in the following sequence? _____

   1, 8, 15, 22, 29, . . .

5. What is the 9th term in the following sequence? _____

   3, 6, 12, 24, . . . *48, 96, 192, 384, 768*

Directions: Use the following table to answer Numbers 6 through 8.

x	y
1	8
4	32
7	56
10	80
13	104

6. What is the rule for the numbers in column x? _____

7. What is the rule for the numbers in column y? _____

8. What is the rule for the pattern going from a number in column x to a number in column y?

   _____

9. Juan had the following number of stolen bases in each of his first five years in Little League.

   4, 9, 14, 19, 24

   If the pattern continues, how many stolen bases will Juan have in his sixth year?

   _____

Functions

A **function** shows a mathematical relationship between two numbers, x and y. In a function, every value of x corresponds to exactly one value of y. An equation is used to represent the relationship between x and y in a function.

 Example

What equation represents the relationship between each x and y in the following table?

x	y
0	10
1	11
2	12
3	13
4	14

First you need to find the rule for the pattern going from a number in column x to a number in column y. The rule is +10. This means that you need to add 10 to each x-value to get a y-value. The following equation can be written to represent the relationship between x and y.

$$y = x + 10$$

 Practice

1. What equation represents the relationship between each x and y in the following table?

x	y
1	−3
3	−1
5	1
7	3
9	5

equation: _____

2. The following equation represents a function.

$$y = \frac{1}{4}x - 1$$

   If the value of x is 32, what is the corresponding value of y? _____

Directions: Use the following table to answer Numbers 3 through 5.

x	y
−2	6
−1	3
0	0
1	−3
2	−6

3. What equation represents the relationship between each x and y in the table?

   _____

4. If the value of x is 18, what is the corresponding value of y? _____

5. If the value of y is −33, what is the corresponding value of x? _____

6. Which set of ordered pairs shows the relationship between x and y in the following function?

   $$y = 5x - 8$$

   A. (2, 2), (4, 12), (5, 17)

   B. (0, −8), (3, 7), (6, 12)

   C. (−1, −13), (1, 3), (8, 32)

   D. (−4, −12), (−3, −7), (7, −7)

Shape Patterns

Sometimes you will see patterns that involve shapes. When trying to identify the order in a shape pattern, analyze the following things.

- the sizes
- the shapes
- the shadings or markings

Example

What is the next figure in the following shape pattern?

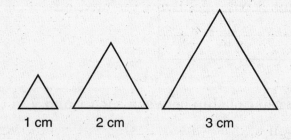

1 cm   2 cm   3 cm

Are the sizes of the figures changing? Yes.

Are the shapes of the figures changing? No.

Are the shadings or markings of the figures changing? No.

All three shapes are triangles. They are increasing in size. The first triangle has sides that are 1 cm long. The second triangle has sides that are 2 cm long. The third triangle has sides that are 3 cm long. The next figure in the pattern is shown below. It is a triangle with sides that are 4 cm long.

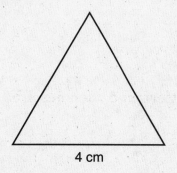

4 cm

 **Practice**

1. Draw the next three figures in the following shape pattern.

2. Each arrangement of dots forms a triangle. Draw the next one.

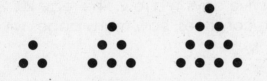

Directions: For Numbers 3 through 6, draw the indicated figures in the following shape pattern.

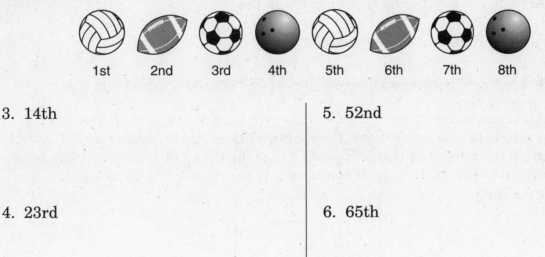

1st 2nd 3rd 4th 5th 6th 7th 8th

3. 14th

4. 23rd

5. 52nd

6. 65th

7. In the space below, draw your own shape pattern and then describe the order of the figures.

_____

_____

103

Achievement Practice

1. A music store has a display of newly released compact discs. Three display racks hold 24 discs. Five display racks hold 40 discs. How many display racks are needed to hold 56 discs?

    A. 9

    B. 8

    C. 7

    D. 6

2. Jan increased her reading each day for five days in a row. She read 20, 25, 31, 38, and then 46 pages. If this pattern continues, how many pages will Jan read on the sixth day?

    A. 56

    B. 55

    C. 54

    D. 53

3. Which equation represents the relationship between x and y in the following table?

x	y
−4	−2
−3	−1
−2	0
−1	1
0	2

    A. $y = x + 2$

    B. $y = x - 2$

    C. $y = 2x$

    D. $y = \frac{1}{2}x$

4. How many squares will appear in row 5 in order to continue the pattern?

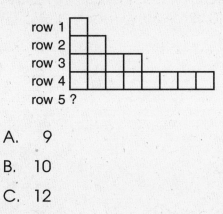

row 1
row 2
row 3
row 4
row 5 ?

A. 9

B. 10

C. 12

D. 16

5. What is the next term in the following pattern?

2, 6, 18, 54, 162, . . .

A. 404

B. 486

C. 566

D. 648

6. Which rule describes the following pattern?

12, 20, 28, 36, 44, . . .

A. add 8

B. subtract 3

C. divide by 9

D. multiply by 6

7. What is the 7th term in the following sequence?

1, −2, 4, −8, . . .

A. 64

B. 32

C. −32

D. −64

8. Which pattern follows the rule +18?

A. 2, 20, 38, 56, 72, . . .

B. 3, 21, 39, 57, 73, . . .

C. 5, 23, 41, 59, 75, . . .

D. 7, 25, 43, 61, 79, . . .

9. The ordered pairs in the following table represent a function.

x	y
10	2
15	3
20	4
25	5
30	6

If the value of x is −5, what is the corresponding value of y?

A. 2

B. 1

C. −1

D. −2

10. What is the 8th term in the following sequence?

10^1, 10^2, 10^4, 10^8, 10^{16}, . . .

A. 10^{40}

B. 10^{96}

C. 10^{128}

D. 10^{256}

11. What are the next two shapes in this pattern?

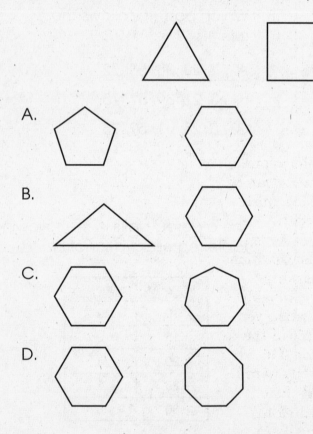

12. In the box below, determine the 10th and 11th terms in the following sequence.

42, 34, 26, 18, 10, . . .

Unit 3

Geometry and Spatial Sense

You might think of geometry as just a classroom activity, but the truth is, geometric concepts can be applied to almost everything you see in the world around you. The natural world is filled with geometric shapes, such as stop signs, soda cans, and cereal boxes. You've performed transformations in math class, but did you realize you perform transformations all the time in real life, probably without even realizing it? For example, when you step in front of a mirror to comb your hair in the morning, the mirror shows your reflection. Or when you ride your bike to school, your tires are performing a series of rotations. Much of the human-made world is constructed according to geometric principles. For example, the walls in your school were made to form right angles with the floor, and the windows were probably placed in carefully measured patterns.

In this unit, you will review points, lines, planes, and angles. You will identify polygons and solids by their properties and view solids from different perspectives. You will also identify and perform transformations of plane figures.

In This Unit
Geometric Concepts

Transformations

Solids

Lesson 8
Geometric Concepts

In this lesson, you will review the basic terms of geometry. You will also identify polygons and solids by their properties and match three-dimensional figures with their two-dimensional representations.

Points, Lines, and Planes

Points, lines, and planes are the basic terms of geometry used to describe and define other terms in geometry.

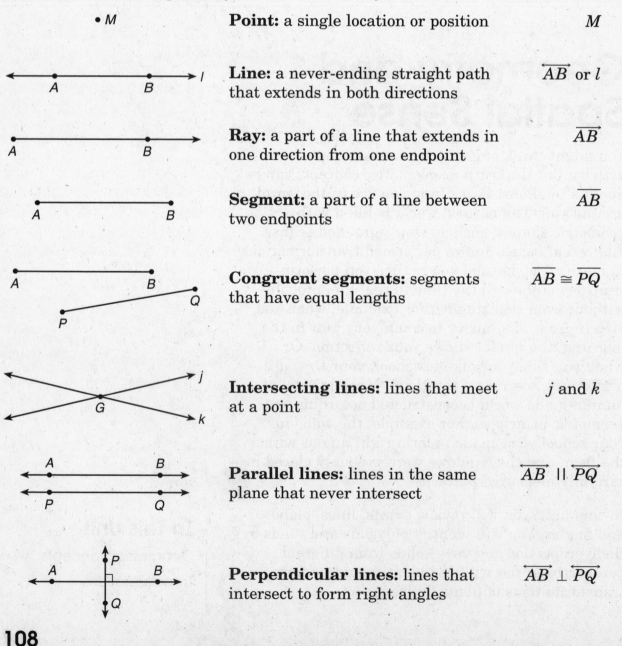

Point: a single location or position · M

M

Line: a never-ending straight path that extends in both directions · $\overleftrightarrow{AB}$ or l

Ray: a part of a line that extends in one direction from one endpoint · $\overrightarrow{AB}$

Segment: a part of a line between two endpoints · $\overline{AB}$

Congruent segments: segments that have equal lengths · $\overline{AB} \cong \overline{PQ}$

Intersecting lines: lines that meet at a point · j and k

Parallel lines: lines in the same plane that never intersect · $\overleftrightarrow{AB} \parallel \overleftrightarrow{PQ}$

Perpendicular lines: lines that intersect to form right angles · $\overleftrightarrow{AB} \perp \overleftrightarrow{PQ}$

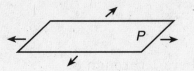

Plane: a set of all points on a flat surface, extending in all directions

P

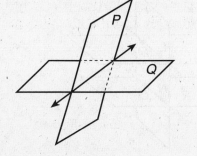

Intersecting planes: planes that meet at a line

P and Q

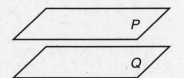

Parallel planes: planes that do not intersect

$P \parallel Q$

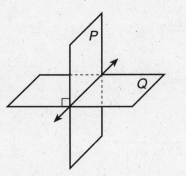

Perpendicular planes: planes that intersect and are at a right angle to each other

$P \perp Q$

Practice

Directions: Use the following figures to complete Numbers 1 through 8.

1. *G* is a _____.

2. $\overline{FD}$ is a _____.

3. $\overleftrightarrow{AB}$ and $\overleftrightarrow{CE}$ are _____ lines.

4. $\overleftrightarrow{AB}$ and $\overleftrightarrow{FG}$ are _____ lines.

5. Where does $\overleftrightarrow{HK}$ intersect *R*? _____

6. Where do *P* and *Q* intersect? _____

7. $\overleftrightarrow{NO}$ is the intersection of _____ and _____.

8. *Q* and *R* are _____ planes.

9. Which of the following represents the intersection of two planes?

   A. line
   B. point
   C. plane
   D. segment

Angles

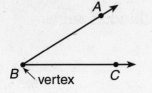

Angle: formed by two rays that share the same endpoint; written as ∠ABC, ∠CBA, or ∠B

Vertex: the endpoint that is shared by two rays that meet to form an angle

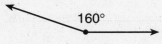

Acute angle: an angle with a measure greater than 0° and less than 90°

Right angle: an angle that measures 90°

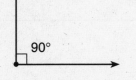

Obtuse angle: an angle with a measure greater than 90° and less than 180°

Straight angle: an angle that measures 180°

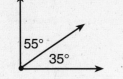

Complementary angles: two angles whose measures have a sum of 90°

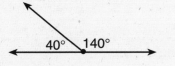

Supplementary angles: two angles whose measures have a sum of 180°

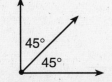

Congruent angles: angles that have the same measure

Practice

Directions: For Numbers 1 through 3, write the name of each kind of angle.

1.

_____

2.

_____

3.

_____

Directions: Use the following figure to answer Numbers 4 through 7.

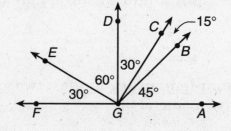

4. Name a straight angle. _____

5. Name a pair of congruent angles. _____

6. Name two complementary angles. _____

7. Name two supplementary angles. _____

Polygons

A **polygon** is a two-dimensional, closed figure that is formed by joining three or more segments at their endpoints.

Triangles

A **triangle** has three angles that are formed by three segments called **sides**. The three endpoints where the segments are joined are the **vertices** of the triangle. A triangle is named by its vertices. Triangles are classified by the types of sides and angles they have. The following table shows the different kinds of triangles. The sides of triangles with the same number of tick marks are congruent. The sum of the measures of the interior angles of a triangle is always 180°.

Types of Triangles

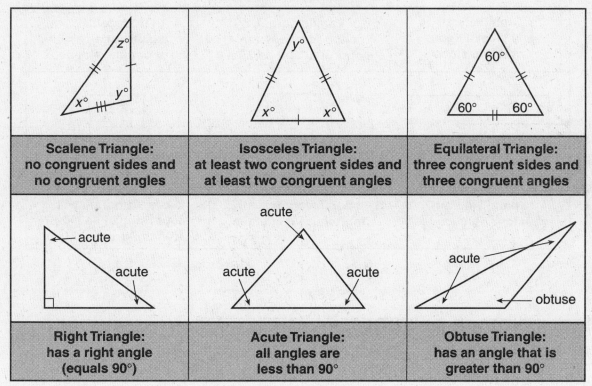

Scalene Triangle: no congruent sides and no congruent angles	Isosceles Triangle: at least two congruent sides and at least two congruent angles	Equilateral Triangle: three congruent sides and three congruent angles
Right Triangle: has a right angle (equals 90°)	Acute Triangle: all angles are less than 90°	Obtuse Triangle: has an angle that is greater than 90°

TIP: A triangle can be classified in more than one way. For example, a triangle can be both acute and isosceles.

Quadrilaterals

A **quadrilateral** has four sides, four angles, and four vertices. Quadrilaterals are classified by the types of sides and angles they have. The following table shows different kinds of quadrilaterals. The sides of quadrilaterals with the same number of arrowheads (> or >>) are parallel. The sides of quadrilaterals with the same number of tick marks are congruent. The sum of the measures of the interior angles of a quadrilateral is always 360°.

Types of Quadrilaterals

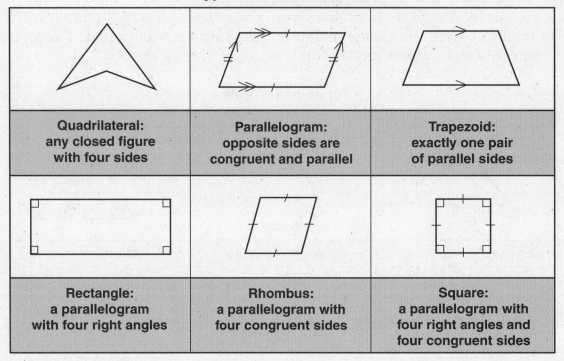

Quadrilateral: any closed figure with four sides	Parallelogram: opposite sides are congruent and parallel	Trapezoid: exactly one pair of parallel sides
Rectangle: a parallelogram with four right angles	Rhombus: a parallelogram with four congruent sides	Square: a parallelogram with four right angles and four congruent sides

Other common polygons

The following table shows other common polygons.

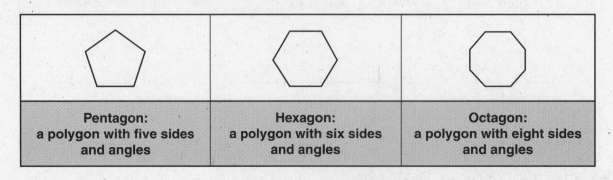

Pentagon: a polygon with five sides and angles	Hexagon: a polygon with six sides and angles	Octagon: a polygon with eight sides and angles

Practice

1. Write the number of all figures that can be described using the names below.

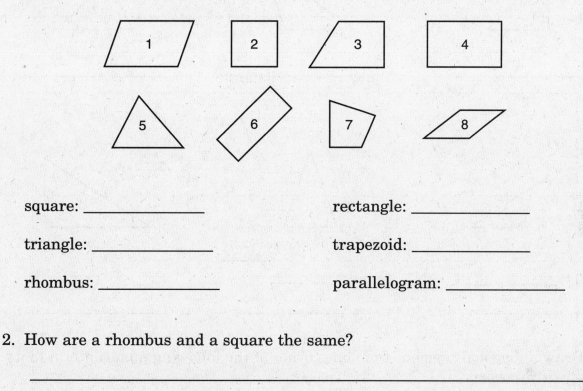

square: _____   rectangle: _____

triangle: _____   trapezoid: _____

rhombus: _____   parallelogram: _____

2. How are a rhombus and a square the same?

   _____

   _____

3. What polygon has exactly one pair of parallel sides? _____

4. Label each triangle below as isosceles, equilateral, or scalene.

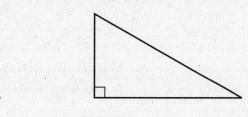 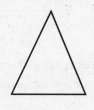

   _____   _____   _____

5. Name a quadrilateral that has four right angles. _____

6. Classify each of the following triangles by writing two of the following words under each triangle: *scalene, isosceles, equilateral, right, acute,* or *obtuse.*

_____   _____   _____

_____   _____   _____

_____   _____   _____

_____   _____   _____

7. Draw a diagonal segment from one corner of the following quadrilateral to its opposite corner.

What is the most specific name for the two polygons that are formed?

_____

8. Which words can be used to describe an equilateral triangle?

   A. acute and scalene

   B. obtuse and scalene

   C. acute and isosceles

   D. obtuse and isosceles

9. Which quadrilateral is **not** a parallelogram?

   A. square

   B. rhombus

   C. rectangle

   D. trapezoid

Circles

A **circle** consists of all points in a plane that are an equal distance from a given point. The radius and diameter describe the size of a circle.

The **radius (r)** is any segment from the center point of the circle to any point on the circle. Radius also refers to the length of that segment. The radius of a circle is half as long as the diameter.

The **diameter (d)** is any segment that passes through the center point of the circle and has both endpoints on the circle. Diameter also refers to the length of that segment. The diameter of a circle is twice as long as the radius.

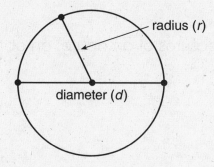

Practice

Directions: Use the following circle to answer Numbers 1 and 2.

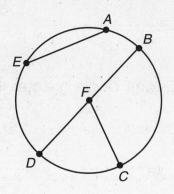

1. What segment represents a radius of the circle? _____

2. What segment represents a diameter of the circle? _____

3. If the radius of a circle is 13 in., how long is the diameter? _____

4. If the diameter of a circle is 54 cm, how long is the radius? _____

Achievement Practice

1. Which drawing shows an obtuse angle?

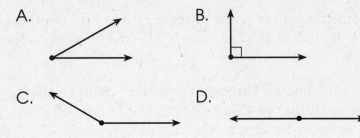

2. Which list shows the measures of an acute, an obtuse, and a right angle, in that order?

    A. 98°, 25°, 90°

    B. 54°, 134°, 80°

    C. 60°, 108°, 90°

    D. 75°, 142°, 100°

3. Name two parallelograms that have four congruent sides.

    _____

4. Which type of triangle has one angle greater than 90° and two sides that are congruent?

    A. right scalene triangle

    B. obtuse isosceles triangle

    C. obtuse scalene triangle

    D. acute isosceles triangle

5. How long is the diameter in the following circle?

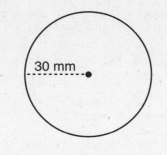

30 mm

A. 10 mm

B. 15 mm

C. 60 mm

D. 90 mm

6. What is the relationship between *A* and *B*?

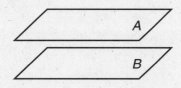

A

B

A. They are parallel.

B. They are perpendicular.

C. They are intersecting.

D. They are supplementary.

7. Which quadrilateral does **not** have opposite angles that are congruent?

A. rectangle

B. rhombus

C. square

D. trapezoid

8. Which drawing shows perpendicular lines?

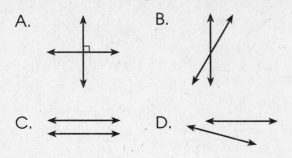

A.   B.

C.   D.

9. Which polygon appears to have at least one right angle?

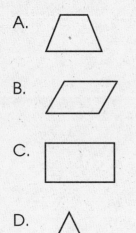

A.

B.

C.

D.

10. Which figure is a polygon but **not** a quadrilateral?

    A. trapezoid

    B. circle

    C. rhombus

    D. triangle

11. If the diameter of a circle is 8 ft, how long is the radius?

    A. 2 ft

    B. 4 ft

    C. 16 ft

    D. 24 ft

12. Which drawing shows complementary angles?

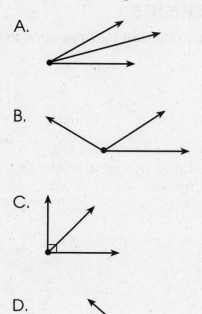

13. What is the name of a plane figure that has the following properties?

    It is a quadrilateral.
    It has opposite sides that are congruent.
    It has opposite sides that are parallel.

    A. circle

    B. parallelogram

    C. trapezoid

    D. pentagon

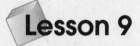

Lesson 9

Transformations

Transformations represent ways in which geometric figures can be moved. In this lesson, you will identify and draw translations, reflections, rotations, and dilations of figures.

Translations, Reflections, and Rotations

A figure that is formed from a translation, reflection, or rotation is congruent to the original figure.

Translations

When a figure is slid without changing anything other than its position, a **translation** has been performed. A figure can be translated in any direction. The following drawing shows three translations of the figure.

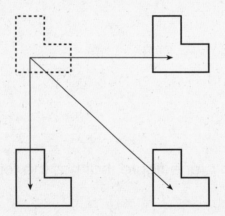

Reflections

When a figure is flipped and its mirror image is created, a **reflection** has been performed. The following drawing shows a reflection of the figure over *y*.

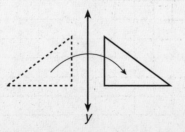

Rotations

When a figure is turned around a fixed point, a **rotation** has been performed. The following drawings show 90°, 180°, 270°, and 360°clockwise rotations of the figure.

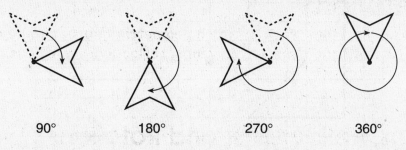

90°   180°   270°   360°

Practice

Directions: For Numbers 1 through 3, write whether the figures show a translation, reflection, or rotation.

1.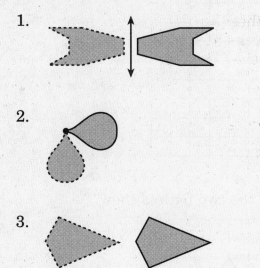

_____

2.

_____

3.

_____

4. On the following grid, draw a translation of the figure.

5. On the following grid, draw a 180°clockwise rotation of the figure around the given point.

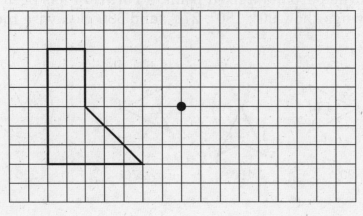

6. On the following grid, draw a reflection of the figure over the given line.

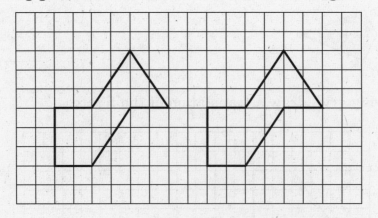

7. On the following grid, what transformation do the two figures show?

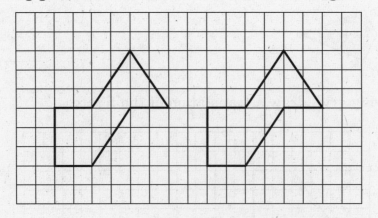

    A. dilation

    B. rotation

    C. reflection

    D. translation

Dilations

When the size of a figure is changed, a **dilation** has been performed. A dilation results in a figure that is **similar** to the original figure. Similar figures have the same shape but not necessarily the same size. The following drawings show two dilations of the first figure.

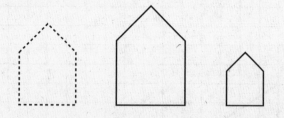

To draw a figure that is similar to a given figure, you multiply each side length of the original figure by a positive number called the **scale factor**. On the following grid, the figure on the left has been dilated using a scale factor of 2 to form the figure on the right.

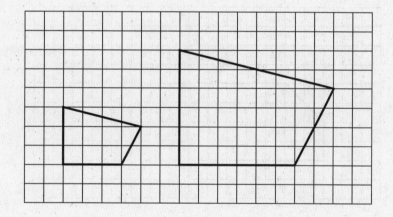

Practice

1. On the following grid, draw a dilation of the figure using a scale factor of 3.

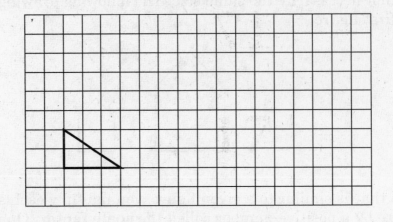

2. On the following grid, draw a dilation of the figure using a scale factor of $\frac{1}{2}$.

3. On the following grid, what scale factor was used to dilate the figure on the left into the figure on the right?

_____

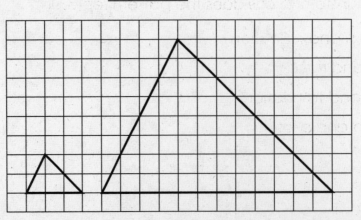

Achievement Practice

1. Ohio became the 17th state in 1803. Which drawing shows a translation?

    A. 17 —→ 17

    B. 17 —→ ⅂Ɩ

    C. 17 —→ ⊥ᘔ

    D. 17 —→ 71

2. Trishelle put a border around her bedroom wall. The border has the following pattern.

    Which two transformations does the pattern represent?

    A. translation and reflection

    B. dilation and rotation

    C. rotation and translation

    D. reflection and dilation

3. If the following figure were reflected over *y*, what would the figure look like?

A.

B.

C.

D.

4. Which drawing shows a dilation of the Ohio state flag?

A.

B.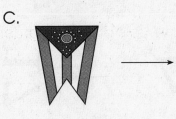

C.

D.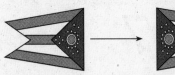

5. On the following grid, draw a 270° clockwise rotation of the figure.

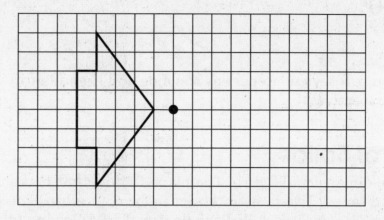

Is the figure you drew congruent to or similar (but not congruent) to the original figure?

_____

6. How many degrees must a figure turn to complete 2 full rotations?

    A. 180°

    B. 360°

    C. 540°

    D. 720°

Lesson 10

Solids

In this lesson, you will review properties of solids and then identify and draw solids from different perspectives.

Properties of Solids

A **solid** is a three-dimensional figure. The plane figures that make the flat surfaces of solids are called **faces**. Two faces intersect to form an **edge**. The point where three or more edges intersect is called the **vertex**. The following table shows some of the different types of solids.

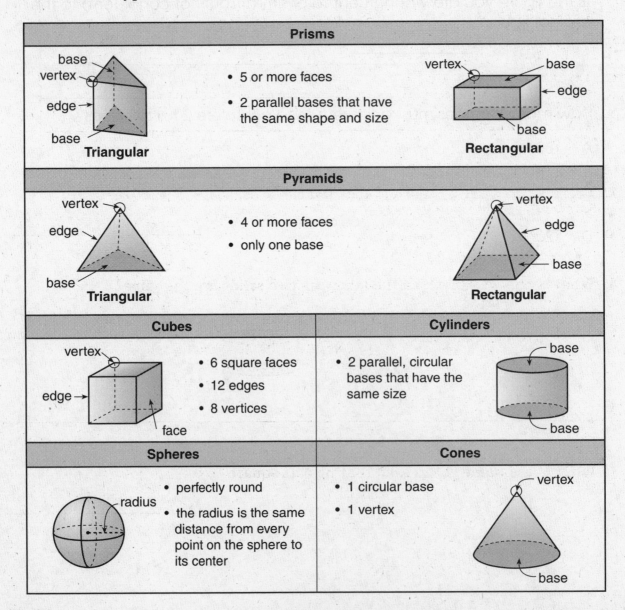

Practice

1. Fill in the following table with the base shape and the number of faces, edges, and vertices that each solid has. Remember, some solids may not have any edges or vertices.

Solid	Base Shape	Faces	Edges	Vertices
Cube				
Cone				
Cylinder				
Triangular Prism				
Rectangular Prism				
Triangular Pyramid				
Rectangular Pyramid				

2. What is the name of the solid that has no faces, edges, or vertices?

_____

3. What is one way in which the following two solids are the same?

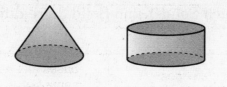

_____

4. What is the name of the solid that has six square faces?

_____

5. What are two ways in which the following solids are the same?

_____

_____

_____

6. Claire cut out four equilateral triangles from a piece of poster board. The triangles are all congruent. If Claire tapes all four triangles together, what solid can she form?

_____

Directions: Use the following solids to answer Numbers 7 through 10.

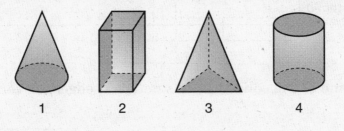

7. What is the name of Solid 4? _____

8. What is one way in which Solid 1 and Solid 3 are different?

_____

_____

9. Which solids have 2 parallel bases?

    A. 1 and 3

    B. 2 and 3

    C. 2 and 4

    D. 3 and 4

10. Which solid has 8 vertices?

    A. 1

    B. 2

    C. 3

    D. 4

Solids from Different Perspectives

When you are given the corner view of a solid, you can draw the front, top, and side views of the solid. Also, when you are given the front, top, and side views of a solid, you can use blocks to build a model of the solid.

 **Example**

Given the following corner view of a solid, draw the front, top, and side views of the solid.

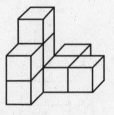

The following drawings show the different views of the solid.

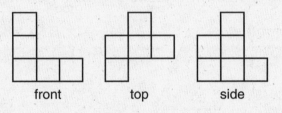

front   top   side

Example

Given the following front, top, and side views of a solid, use blocks to build a model of the solid.

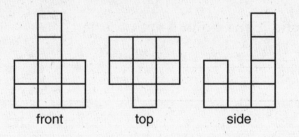

front   top   side

The following solid can be built using blocks.

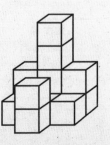

Practice

Directions: For Numbers 1 through 4, write the letter of the front, top, and side views that match the corner view of each solid.

1.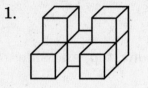

A.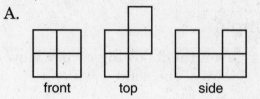

_____

2.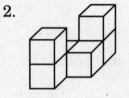

B.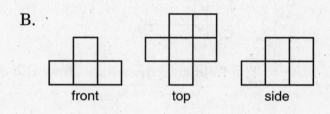

_____

3.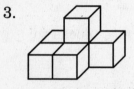

C.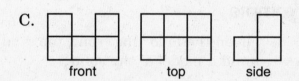

_____

4.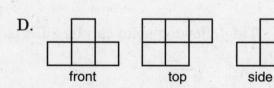

D.

_____

Directions: For Numbers 5 through 7, draw and label the front, top, and side views of the given solid.

5.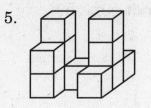

6.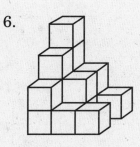

7.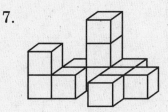

8. Use blocks to build a solid that has the following front, top, and side views.

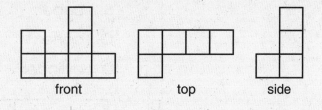

front   top   side

Achievement Practice

1. Which solid does **not** have at least one triangular face?

   A. cone

   B. square pyramid

   C. triangular pyramid

   D. triangular prism

2. How many faces, edges, and vertices does a square pyramid have?

   A. 4 faces, 6 edges, 4 vertices

   B. 5 faces, 4 edges, 4 vertices

   C. 5 faces, 8 edges, 5 vertices

   D. 6 faces, 12 edges, 8 vertices

3. How many faces does a rectangular prism have?

   A. 2

   B. 4

   C. 6

   D. 8

4. Which solid is **not** a prism?

   A.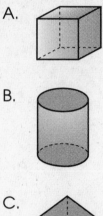

   B.

   C.

   D.

5. What is the name of the solid that has two circular bases?

   A. sphere

   B. cube

   C. cone

   D. cylinder

6. What does the top view of the following solid look like?

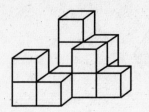

A.

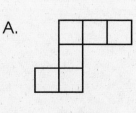

B.

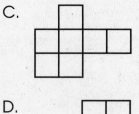

C.

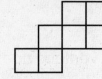

D.

7. Which is not the front, top, or side view of the following solid?

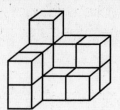

A.

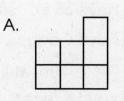

B.

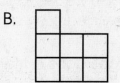

C.

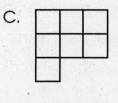

D.

8. Which statement about the following two solids is true?

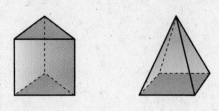

   A. They both have 6 vertices.

   B. They both have 9 edges.

   C. They both have 2 triangular bases.

   D. They both have 5 faces.

9. How many edges does a triangular pyramid have?

   A. 4

   B. 6

   C. 8

   D. 9

10. What is the name of the following solid, and how many vertices does it have?

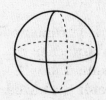

    name: _____

    vertices: _____

Unit 4

Measurement

Just about everything in the world around you that is made by people had its start in mathematical concepts of measurement. Buildings, clothing, and bicycles were all made with precise measurements. Even music and computer games involve some incredibly complex and amazing measurements. (Did you know, for example, that the spiral track that contains the information on a compact disc is more than 3.5 miles long?) Measurement skills also play an important part in most jobs. For example, airplane navigators must measure angles very accurately to keep their planes on course.

In this unit, you will review your measurement skills by converting from one unit to another within the same measurement system. You will measure angles and find the perimeter and area of polygons, and the circumference and area of circles. You will also find the surface area and volume of solids.

In This Unit
Measurement Systems
Geometric Measurement

Lesson 11

Measurement Systems

In this lesson, you will convert from one unit of measurement to another using proportions and algebra.

Units of Length

The units of length in the U.S. customary system that you should be familiar with are **inches (in.)**, **feet (ft)**, **yards (yd)**, and **miles (mi)**. In the metric system, the units you should be familiar with are **millimeters (mm)**, **centimeters (cm)**, **meters (m)**, and **kilometers (km)**.

U.S. customary system

To help you set up the correct proportions for converting U.S. customary units of length, use these unit conversions.

> 1 ft = 12 in.   1 yd = 3 ft   1 yd = 36 in.   1 mi = 1,760 yd   1 mi = 5,280 ft

Example

Convert 11 feet to inches.

Use the conversion that relates feet and inches: 1 ft = 12 in.

Set up a proportion. Write the conversion as a ratio and let x be the unknown.

$$\frac{1 \text{ ft}}{12 \text{ in.}} = \frac{11 \text{ ft}}{x}$$

Ignore the units for now and cross multiply.

$$\frac{1}{12} = \frac{11}{x}$$

$$1 \cdot x = 11 \cdot 12$$

$$x = 132$$

The answer is 11 ft = 132 in.

Practice

Directions: For Numbers 1 through 10, set up a proportion and make the conversion.

1. 10 yd = _____ ft

6. 3 mi = _____ yd

2. 96 in. = _____ ft

7. 72 ft = _____ yd

3. 2 yd = _____ in.

8. 21,120 ft = _____ mi

4. 1 ft = _____ in.

9. 216 in. = _____ yd

5. 3 yd = ?

   A. 108 in.

   B. 112 in.

   C. 120 in.

   D. 144 in.

10. 84 in. = ?

   A. 8 ft

   B. 7 ft

   C. 6 ft

   D. 5 ft

Metric system

To help you set up the correct proportions for converting metric units of length, use these unit conversions.

$$1 \text{ cm} = 10 \text{ mm} \qquad 1 \text{ m} = 100 \text{ cm} \qquad 1 \text{ m} = 1,000 \text{ mm} \qquad 1 \text{ km} = 1,000 \text{ m}$$

 **Example**

Convert 2,300 meters to kilometers.

Use the conversion that relates meters and kilometers: 1 km = 1,000 m.

Set up a proportion. Write the conversion as a ratio and let x be the unknown.

$$\frac{1 \text{ km}}{1,000 \text{ m}} = \frac{x}{2,300 \text{ m}}$$

Ignore the units for now and cross multiply.

$$\frac{1}{1,000} = \frac{x}{2,300}$$

$$1,000 \cdot x = 1 \cdot 2,300$$

$$x = 2.3$$

The answer is 2,300 m = 2.3 km.

Practice

Directions: For Numbers 1 through 10, set up a proportion and make the conversion.

1. 60 m = _____ cm

2. 15,000 m = _____ km

3. 20 cm = _____ mm

4. 0.05 m = _____ cm

5. 90 m = ?

   A.   9 mm

   B.   900 mm

   C. 9,000 mm

   D. 90,000 mm

6. 4 km = _____ cm

7. 16,000 mm = _____ m

8. 122 cm = _____ mm

9. 62 km = _____ m

10. 30 cm = ?

    A. 0.03 m

    B. 0.3 m

    C. 3 m

    D. 30 m

Units of Weight

The units of weight in the U.S. customary system that you should be familiar with are **ounces (oz)**, **pounds (lb)**, and **tons (T)**. In the metric system, the units you should be familiar with are **milligrams (mg)**, **grams (g)**, and **kilograms (kg)**.

U.S. customary system

To help you set up the correct proportions for converting U.S. customary units of weight, use these unit conversions.

$$1 \text{ lb} = 16 \text{ oz} \qquad 1 \text{ T} = 2{,}000 \text{ lb} \qquad 1 \text{ T} = 32{,}000 \text{ oz}$$

 **Example**

Convert 8 pounds to ounces.

Use the conversion that relates pounds and ounces: 1 lb = 16 oz.

Set up a proportion. Write the conversion as a ratio and let x be the unknown.

$$\frac{1 \text{ lb}}{16 \text{ oz}} = \frac{8 \text{ lb}}{x}$$

Ignore the units for now and cross multiply.

$$\frac{1}{16} = \frac{8}{x}$$

$$1 \cdot x = 16 \cdot 8$$

$$x = 128$$

The answer is 8 lb = 128 oz.

Practice

Directions: For Numbers 1 through 10, set up a proportion and make the conversion.

1. 144 oz = _____ lb

2. 5 T = _____ lb

3. 64,000 oz = _____ T

4. 88 oz = _____ lb

5. 0.5 T = ?

   A. 1,000 lb
   B. 2,000 lb
   C. 3,000 lb
   D. 4,000 lb

6. 192 oz = _____ lb

7. 8,000 lb = _____ T

8. 2.5 lb = _____ oz

9. 3 T = _____ oz

10. 24 lb = ?

    A. 192 oz
    B. 288 oz
    C. 384 oz
    D. 432 oz

Metric system

To help you set up the correct proportions for converting metric units of weight, use these unit conversions.

$$1 \text{ g} = 1,000 \text{ mg} \qquad 1 \text{ kg} = 1,000 \text{ g} \qquad 1 \text{ kg} = 1,000,000 \text{ mg}$$

Example

Convert 24,000 grams to kilograms.

Use the conversion that relates grams and kilograms: 1 kg = 1,000 g.

Set up a proportion. Write the conversion as a ratio and let x be the unknown.

$$\frac{1 \text{ kg}}{1,000 \text{ g}} = \frac{x}{24,000 \text{ g}}$$

Ignore the units for now and cross multiply.

$$\frac{1}{1,000} = \frac{x}{24,000}$$

$$1,000 \cdot x = 1 \cdot 24,000$$

$$x = 24$$

The answer is 24,000 g = 24 kg.

Practice

Directions: For Numbers 1 through 10, set up a proportion and make the conversion.

1. 4 g = _____ mg

2. 2,500 mg = _____ g

3. 8 kg = _____ mg

4. 5,000 g = _____ kg

5. 10,000 mg = ?

    A.   1 g

    B.   10 g

    C.   100 g

    D. 1,000 g

6. 3.5 kg = _____ mg

7. 500 g = _____ kg

8. 90 g = _____ mg

9. 7,000 mg = _____ g

10. 6,200 g = ?

    A.   0.62 kg

    B.   6.2 kg

    C. 62 kg

    D. 620 kg

Units of Capacity

The units of capacity in the U.S. customary system that you should be familiar with are **fluid ounces (fl oz)**, **cups (c)**, **pints (pt)**, **quarts (qt)**, and **gallons (gal)**. In the metric system, the units you should be familiar with are **milliliters (mL)**, **liters (L)**, and **kiloliters (kL)**.

U.S. customary system

To help you set up the correct proportions for converting U.S. customary units of capacity, use these unit conversions.

$1 \text{ c} = 8 \text{ fl oz}$ $1 \text{ pt} = 2 \text{ c}$ $1 \text{ pt} = 16 \text{ fl oz}$ $1 \text{ qt} = 2 \text{ pt}$ $1 \text{ qt} = 4 \text{ c}$

$1 \text{ qt} = 32 \text{ fl oz}$ $1 \text{ gal} = 4 \text{ qt}$ $1 \text{ gal} = 8 \text{ pt}$ $1 \text{ gal} = 16 \text{ c}$ $1 \text{ gal} = 128 \text{ fl oz}$

Example

Convert 18 quarts to cups.

Use the conversion that relates quarts and cups: $1 \text{ qt} = 4 \text{ c}$.

Set up a proportion. Write the conversion as a ratio and let x be the unknown.

$$\frac{1 \text{ qt}}{4 \text{ c}} = \frac{18 \text{ qt}}{x}$$

Ignore the units for now and cross multiply.

$$\frac{1}{4} = \frac{18}{x}$$

$$1 \cdot x = 4 \cdot 18$$

$$x = 72$$

The answer is $18 \text{ qt} = 72 \text{ c}$.

Practice

Directions: For Numbers 1 through 10, set up a proportion and make the conversion.

1. 7 c = _____ fl oz

2. 15 qt = _____ pt

3. 64 fl oz = _____ pt

4. 5 gal = _____ pt

5. 92 c = ?

   A. 12 qt

   B. 23 qt

   C. 30 qt

   D. 46 qt

6. 256 fl oz = _____ qt

7. 48 pt = _____ c

8. 4 gal = _____ fl oz

9. 80 c = _____ gal

10. 100 qt = ?

    A. 20 gal

    B. 25 gal

    C. 35 gal

    D. 50 gal

Metric system

To help you set up the correct proportions for converting metric units of capacity, use these unit conversions.

$$1\text{ L} = 1{,}000\text{ mL} \qquad 1\text{ kL} = 1{,}000\text{ L} \qquad 1\text{ kL} = 1{,}000{,}000\text{ mL}$$

Example

Convert 8.8 kiloliters to liters.

Use the conversion that relates kiloliters and liters: 1 kL = 1,000 L.

Set up a proportion. Write the conversion as a ratio and let x be the unknown.

$$\frac{1\text{ kL}}{1{,}000\text{ L}} = \frac{8.8\text{ kL}}{x}$$

Ignore the units for now and cross multiply.

$$\frac{1}{1{,}000} = \frac{8.8}{x}$$

$$1 \cdot x = 1{,}000 \cdot 8.8$$

$$x = 8{,}800$$

The answer is 8.8 kL = 8,800 L.

 Practice

Directions: For Numbers 1 through 10, set up a proportion and make the conversion.

1. 25 L = _____ mL

2. 2 kL = _____ L

3. 5,000 mL = _____ kL

4. 28,000 L = _____ kL

5. 1,600 mL = ?

   A. 160 L

   B. 16 L

   C. 1.6 L

   D. 0.16 L

6. 10 kL = _____ L

7. 0.9 kL = _____ mL

8. 6 L = _____ mL

9. 4,000 L = _____ kL

10. 2 kL = ?

   A. 2,000 mL

   B. 20,000 mL

   C. 200,000 mL

   D. 2,000,000 mL

Units of Time

The units of time are the same in the U.S. customary system and the metric system. The units of time you should be familiar with are **seconds (s)**, **minutes (min)**, **hours (hr)**, **days (d)**, **weeks (wk)**, **months (mo)**, and **years (yr)**.

To help you set up the correct proportions for converting units of time, use these unit conversions.

$$1 \text{ min} = 60 \text{ s} \qquad 1 \text{ hr} = 60 \text{ min} \qquad 1 \text{ hr} = 3{,}600 \text{ s} \qquad 1 \text{ d} = 24 \text{ hr}$$

$$1 \text{ d} = 1{,}440 \text{ min} \qquad 1 \text{ wk} = 7 \text{ d} \qquad 1 \text{ wk} = 168 \text{ hr} \qquad 1 \text{ yr} = 12 \text{ mo}$$

$$1 \text{ yr} = 52 \text{ wk} \qquad 1 \text{ yr} = 365 \text{ d} \quad \text{(Leap years have 366 days.)}$$

 **Example**

Convert 9 hours to minutes.

Use the conversion that relates hours and minutes: 1 hr = 60 min.

Set up a proportion. Write the conversion as a ratio and let x be the unknown.

$$\frac{1 \text{ hr}}{60 \text{ min}} = \frac{9 \text{ hr}}{x}$$

Ignore the units for now and cross multiply.

$$\frac{1}{60} = \frac{9}{x}$$

$$1 \cdot x = 60 \cdot 9$$

$$x = 540$$

The answer is 9 hr = 540 min.

 TIP: Leap years are divisible by 4. The years 2004, 2008, 2012, and so on are leap years.

152

Practice

Directions: For Numbers 1 through 10, set up a proportion and make the conversion.

1. 3 yr = _____ wk

2. 180 min = _____ hr

3. 840 hr = _____ wk

4. 10 yr = _____ mo

5. 2 hr = ?

   A. 1,200 s

   B. 3,600 s

   C. 7,200 s

   D. 12,000 s

6. 15 min = _____ s

7. 2 d = _____ min

8. 10 yr = _____ hr
   (Include 2 leap years.)

9. 6 d = _____ hr

10. 510 min = ?

    A. 8 hr

    B. 8.5 hr

    C. 9 hr

    D. 9.5 hr

Achievement Practice

1. How do you convert mL to L?

   A. divide by 100

   B. divide by 1,000

   C. multiply by 100

   D. multiply by 1,000

2. Janice used 2 rolls of transparent tape that were each 168 in. long for wrapping packages. How many feet of tape did she use?

   A. 28

   B. 24

   C. 18

   D. 14

3. Dr. Vile is raising a man-eating plant in his laboratory. Right now, the plant is 0.6 ft tall. **About** how tall is the plant in inches?

   A. 3 in.

   B. 7 in.

   C. 9 in.

   D. 11 in.

4. Kurt ran $\frac{1}{2}$ mi as part of soccer practice on each of 3 days. Which is the most reasonable estimate for the distance he ran in feet?

   A. 2,600 ft

   B. 5,500 ft

   C. 7,200 ft

   D. 7,800 ft

5. How many pints are in 5 gallons?

   A. 20 pt

   B. 30 pt

   C. 40 pt

   D. 50 pt

6. Which conversion can be made by multiplying by 10?

   A. cm to mm

   B. m to km

   C. m to cm

   D. mm to km

7. A cement mixer poured out 5,000 lb of cement. How many tons did the cement weigh?

   A. 2 T

   B. 2.25 T

   C. 2.5 T

   D. 2.75 T

8. A basketball player is 83 in. tall. What is the player's height in feet and inches?

   A. 7 ft, 2 in.

   B. 6 ft, 9 in.

   C. 7 ft, 4 in.

   D. 6 ft, 11 in.

9. Dennis has a 16-ft–long pipe. How many inches long is the pipe?

   A.   48 in.

   B. 160 in.

   C. 182 in.

   D. 192 in.

10. Emily practiced the piano for a total of $6\frac{1}{2}$ hours this week. How many minutes did she practice?

    A. 360 min

    B. 390 min

    C. 410 min

    D. 420 min

11. 336 fl oz = ?

    A. 10.5 qt

    B. 11.2 qt

    C. 12 qt

    D. 14 qt

12. Which conversion is correct?

    A. 2 yd = 8 ft

    B. 7 lb = 56 oz

    C. 5 gal = 10 qt

    D. 8 hr = 480 min

13. Which statement is true?

    A. A quarter-pound hamburger weighs 3 oz.

    B. A 0.5-L jar will be completely filled by 5 mL of liquid.

    C. A 50-cm–long toy car has the same length as one that is 0.5 m long.

    D. A kilogram of lead weighs as much as 100 g of feathers.

14. Dr. Garvey was principal of Foreman High School for 12 years. How many months was he principal?

    A. 72 mo

    B. 132 mo

    C. 144 mo

    D. 156 mo

15. Tommy's dog weighs 19.5 kg. What is the weight of Tommy's dog in grams and milligrams?

    _____ g

    _____ mg

Lesson 12

Geometric Measurement

In this lesson, you will measure angles and find the sum of the angle measures of polygons. You will also review perimeter, area, surface area, and volume.

Perimeter

Perimeter (P) is the distance around the outside of a two-dimensional figure. This distance is called the **circumference (C)** when the two-dimensional figure is a circle. The following table shows formulas for finding the perimeters and circumferences of different two-dimensional figures.

Figure	Formula	
polygon	$P = s_1 + s_2 + s_3 + \ldots + s_n$	where s_n = length of side n n = number of sides
regular polygon	$P = l \cdot$ number of sides	where l = length of each side
square	$P = 4s$	where s = length of each side
rectangle	$P = 2l + 2w$ or $P = 2(l + w)$	where l = length w = width
circle	$C = \pi d$ or $C = 2\pi r$	where d = diameter r = radius $\pi \approx 3.14$

TIP: The numbers to the right of and lower than the letters are called subscripts. They are used to show the different sides of polygons: s_1 means side 1, s_2 means side 2, and so on.

**Example**

What is the perimeter of this rectangle?

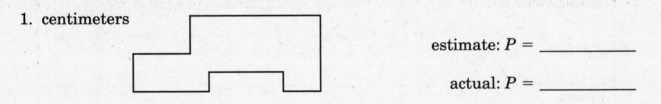

2 ft

7 ft

$$P = 2l + 2w$$
$$= 2 \cdot 7 + 2 \cdot 2$$
$$= 18$$

The perimeter of the rectangle is 18 ft.

Practice

Directions: For Numbers 1 and 2, estimate the perimeter or circumference of the shape using the given units. Then measure the actual perimeter or circumference.

1. centimeters

estimate: $P =$ _____

actual: $P =$ _____

2. inches

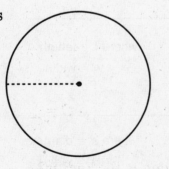

estimate: $C =$ _____

actual: $C =$ _____

Directions: For Numbers 3 and 4, find the perimeter of each shape.

3. 4 in.   9 in.   12 in.

P = _____

4. 6 m   3 m   3 m   6 m   10 m

P = _____

5. What is the perimeter of a rectangle that has a length of 12 mm and a width of 11 mm?

P = _____

Directions: For Numbers 6 and 7, find the circumference of each circle.

6. 8 in.

C = _____

7. 10 mm

C = _____

8. If the circumference of a circle is 94.2 yd, how long is the radius?

r = _____

Area

Area (*A*) is the measure of the region inside a two-dimensional figure. Area is measured in square units. The following table shows formulas for finding the areas of different two-dimensional figures.

Figure	Formula
triangle	$A = \frac{1}{2}bh$ where *b* = base length *h* = height
square	$A = s^2$ where *s* = length of each side
rectangle	$A = lw$ where *l* = length *w* = width
parallelogram	$A = bh$ where *b* = base length *h* = height
trapezoid	$A = \frac{1}{2}h(b_1 + b_2)$ where b_1 = base 1 length b_2 = base 2 length *h* = height
circle	$A = \pi r^2$ where *r* = radius $\pi \approx 3.14$

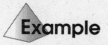 Example

What is the area of this parallelogram?

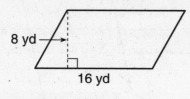

8 yd

16 yd

A = bh

= 16 • 8

= 128

The area of the parallelogram is 128 yd².

Practice

Directions: For Numbers 1 and 2, estimate the area of the shape in cm². Then measure the actual area.

☐ = 1 cm²

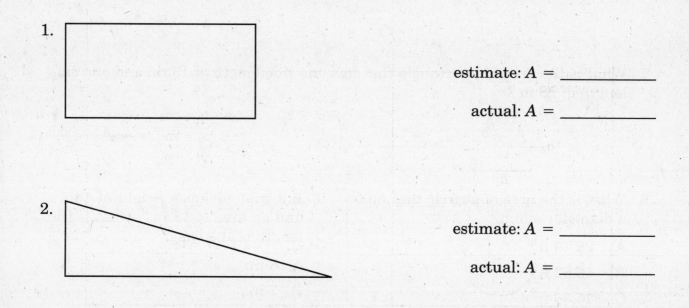

1.

estimate: A = _____

actual: A = _____

2.

estimate: A = _____

actual: A = _____

Directions: For Numbers 3 through 6, find the area of each shape.

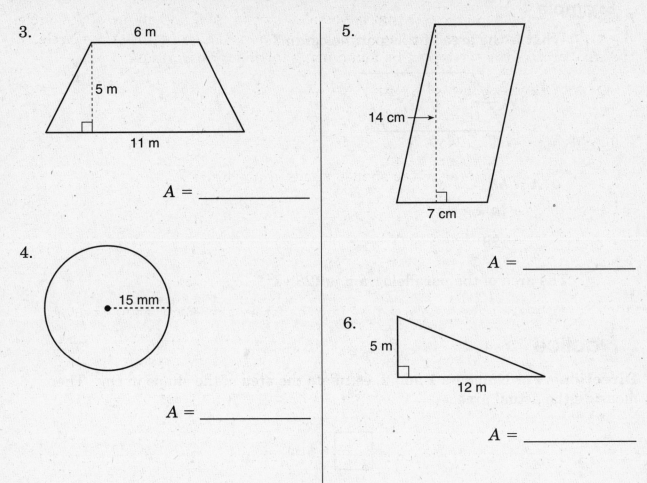

3. 6 m

    5 m

    11 m

    A = _____

4. 15 mm

    A = _____

5. 14 cm →

    7 cm

    A = _____

6. 5 m

    12 m

    A = _____

7. What is the area of a rectangle that has one side length of 13 in. and one side length of 28 in.?

    A = _____

8. What is the area of a circle that has a diameter of 6 ft?

    A. 28.26 ft^2

    B. 56.52 ft^2

    C. 75.36 ft^2

    D. 113.04 ft^2

9. If a triangle has a height of 4 in. and an area of 18 in.^{2}, what is the length of the base?

    A. 6 in.

    B. 7 in.

    C. 8 in.

    D. 9 in.

Area of sectors

A **sector** is a region of a circle that is bounded by two radii and an arc of the circle. If x represents the measure of the arc of a sector and r is the radius of the circle, then the area of the sector can be found using the following formula.

$$\text{area of the sector} = \frac{x}{360} \cdot \pi r^2$$

Example

What is the area of the shaded sector of this circle?

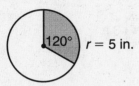 $r = 5$ in.

Substitute the known values into the formula for the area of a sector.

$$\text{area of the sector} = \frac{x}{360} \cdot \pi r^2$$

$$= \frac{120}{360} \cdot 3.14 \cdot 5^2$$

$$= 26.16666\ldots$$

The area of the shaded sector is about 26 in.^{2}.

Practice

Directions: For Numbers 1 through 3, find the area of the shaded sector to the nearest whole number.

1. 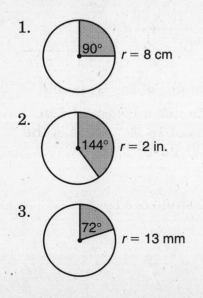 $r = 8$ cm

A = _____

2. $144°$ $r = 2$ in.

A = _____

3. $72°$ $r = 13$ mm

A = _____

Comparing Perimeters and Areas

Two different figures with the same perimeter may have different areas. Also, two figures with different perimeters may have the same area.

Example

Find the perimeters and areas of the following square and rectangle.

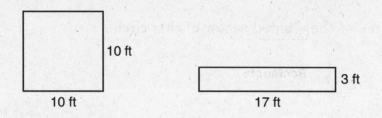

The perimeter of the square is 40 ft. The perimeter of the rectangle is also 40 ft.

The area of the square is 100 ft^2. The area of the rectangle is 51 ft^2.

The two figures have the same perimeter but different areas.

Example

Find the perimeters and areas of the following triangle and trapezoid.

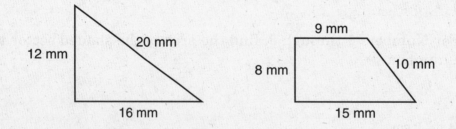

The perimeter of the triangle is 48 mm. The perimeter of the trapezoid is 42 mm.

The area of the triangle is 96 mm^2. The area of the trapezoid is also 96 mm^2.

The two figures have different perimeters but the same area.

Practice

Directions: Use the following rectangles to answer Numbers 1 through 4.

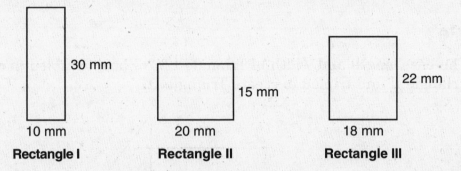

1. Which two rectangles have the same perimeter? _____

2. Which two rectangles have the same area? _____

3. If you drew a square with the same perimeter as that of Rectangle II, what would be the length of each side?

   _____

4. In the space provided below, use a ruler to draw a right triangle with the same area as that of Rectangle III.

5. Do the following figures have the same perimeter, the same area, or the same perimeter **and** same area?

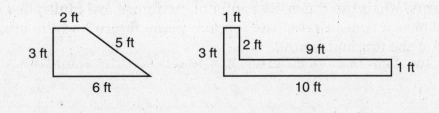

Change in Dimensions

When the dimensions of a plane figure are changed proportionally, you can see how the perimeter and area of the new figure compare to those of the original figure.

 **Example**

The base length and width of Triangle I have been doubled to create Triangle II and tripled to create Triangle III.

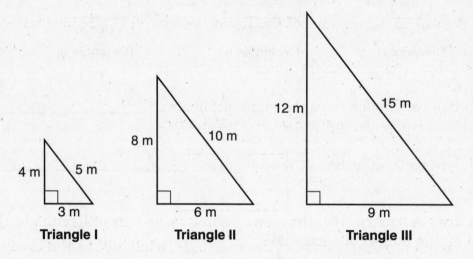

	Triangle I	Triangle II	Triangle III
Triangle I	4 m, 5 m, 3 m		
Triangle II	8 m, 10 m, 6 m		
Triangle III	12 m, 15 m, 9 m		

The following table shows the perimeters and areas of Triangles I, II, and III.

	Triangle I	Triangle II	Triangle III
Perimeter	12 m	24 m	36 m
Area	6 m^2	24 m^2	54 m^2

The table shows that when the base length and height of a triangle are doubled, the perimeter doubles and the area becomes 2^2 or 4 times greater. When the base length and height are tripled, the perimeter triples and the area becomes 3^2 or 9 times greater.

In general terms, when the dimensions of a plane figure are multiplied by n, the perimeter becomes n times that of the original plane figure and the area becomes n^2 times that of the original figure.

Practice

1. The perimeter of the following figure is 16 cm.

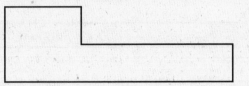

   If you triple the dimensions of the figure, what will be the perimeter of the new figure?

   _____

2. The area of the following rectangle is 450 mm^2.

   If you double the dimensions of the rectangle, what will be the area of the new rectangle?

   _____

3. If the radius of a circle is multiplied by 4, how will the area change?

   _____

4. If each side length of a parallelogram is multiplied by 6, how will the perimeter change?

   _____

5. If the side length of a square is multiplied by 5, how will the area change?

   A. It will become 5 times greater.

   B. It will become 10 times greater.

   C. It will become 20 times greater.

   D. It will become 25 times greater.

Surface Area

Surface area (SA) is the measure of the outside of a solid. Surface area is measured in square units. The following table shows formulas for finding the surface areas of different solids.

Figure	Formula	
prism 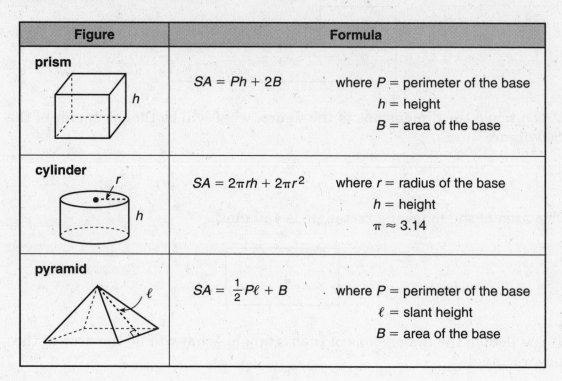	$SA = Ph + 2B$	where P = perimeter of the base h = height B = area of the base
cylinder	$SA = 2\pi rh + 2\pi r^2$	where r = radius of the base h = height $\pi \approx 3.14$
pyramid	$SA = \frac{1}{2}P\ell + B$	where P = perimeter of the base ℓ = slant height B = area of the base

Example

What is the surface area of this rectangular pyramid?

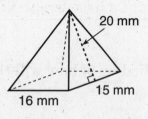

20 mm
15 mm
16 mm

Substitute the values into the following formula.

$$SA = \frac{1}{2}P\ell + B$$

$$= \frac{1}{2} \cdot (2 \cdot 16 + 2 \cdot 15) \cdot 20 + 15 \cdot 16$$

$$= 860$$

The surface area of the rectangular pyramid is 860 mm^2.

Practice

Directions: For Numbers 1 through 3, find the surface area of each solid.

1.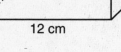
   r = 2 ft
   7 ft

   SA = _____

2.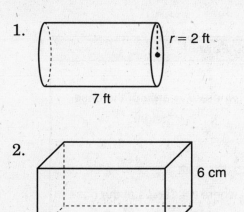
   6 cm
   3 cm
   12 cm

   SA = _____

3.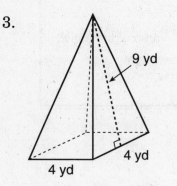
   9 yd
   4 yd
   4 yd

   SA = _____

4. What is the surface area of a square pyramid with a base length of 20 mm and a slant height of 11 mm?

   SA = _____

5. What is the surface area of a cylinder that has a diameter of 17 in. and a height of 6 in.?

   A. 546.36 in.^{2}

   B. 640.56 in.^{2}

   C. 774.01 in.^{2}

   D. 867.43 in.^{2}

6. If a cube has a surface area of 384 m^2, what is its side length?

   A. 6 m

   B. 7 m

   C. 8 m

   D. 9 m

Volume

Volume (V) is the amount of space inside a solid. Volume is measured in cubic units. The following table shows formulas for finding the volumes of different solids.

Figure	Formula	
prism 	$V = Bh$	where B = area of the base h = height
cylinder 	$V = \pi r^2 h$	where r = radius of the base h = height $\pi \approx 3.14$
pyramid 	$V = \frac{1}{3} Bh$	where B = area of the base h = height

◤ **Example**

What is the volume of this cylinder?

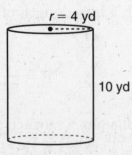

Substitute the values into the following formula.

$$V = \pi r^2 h$$

$$= 3.14 \cdot 4^2 \cdot 10$$

$$= 502.4$$

The volume of the cylinder is 502.4 yd³.

Practice

Directions: For Numbers 1 through 3, find the volume of each solid.

1.

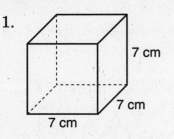

7 cm

7 cm

7 cm

V = _____

2.

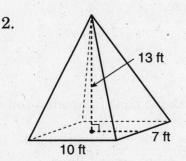

13 ft

7 ft

10 ft

V = _____

3.

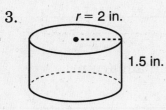

r = 2 in.

1.5 in.

V = _____

4. What is the volume of a cylinder that has a diameter of 2 yd and a height of 12 yd?

V = _____

5. What is the volume of a square pyramid that has a base length of 5 m and a height of 15 m?

A. 125 m³

B. 225 m³

C. 275 m³

D. 375 m³

6. If a rectangular prism has a length of 18 mm, a width of 9 mm, and a volume of 3,240 mm³, what is the height?

A. 14 mm

B. 16 mm

C. 18 mm

D. 20 mm

Choosing the Correct Measure

When you are given a problem situation involving geometric measurement, you need to decide whether perimeter, area, surface area, or volume is the correct measure to use to solve the problem.

 **Example**

Which measure would you use to determine the amount of wrapping paper you need to wrap a box?

Since you need to determine the total area on the outside surface of the box, surface area would be the best measure to use.

 **Practice**

Directions: For Numbers 1 through 5, determine the measure that is needed for each problem situation.

1. Determining the amount of carpet you need to cover the basement floor.

   _____

2. Determining the amount of water you need to fill your fish aquarium.

   _____

3. Determining the number of bricks you need to border your flower bed.

   _____

4. Determining the amount of paint you need for the outside of a house.

   _____

5. Determining the amount of ice cream that will fit inside an ice cream cone.

   _____

Achievement Practice

1. What is the area of the shaded sector of this circle? Round your answer to the nearest tenth.

    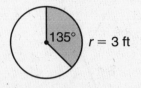

    A.   9.4 ft²

    B.   10.6 ft²

    C.   11.4 ft²

    D.   12.7 ft²

2. How much sand will fit inside this sandbox?

    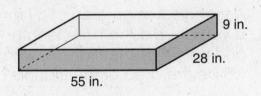

    A.   510 in.³

    B.   1,540 in.³

    C.   4,620 in.³

    D.   13,860 in.³

3. Leroy's bicycle tires are 34 in. in diameter. How far will the bike travel in exactly one full turn of the tires?

    A.   53.38 in.

    B.   106.76 in.

    C.   160.14 in.

    D.   213.52 in.

4. What is the area of a trapezoid that has base lengths of 12 in. and 14 in. and a height of 13 in.?

    A.   195 in.²

    B.   182 in.²

    C.   169 in.²

    D.   156 in.²

5. Sylvester wants to determine the length of trim he needs to put around the picture window in his living room. Which measure does Sylvester need to use?

    A.   volume

    B.   surface area

    C.   perimeter

    D.   area

6. The world's largest basket is in Newark, Ohio. The base of the basket is 64 yd long and 42 yd wide. What is the area of the base of this basket?

   A. 2,568 yd^2

   B. 2,668 yd^2

   C. 2,688 yd^2

   D. 2,698 yd^2

7. What is the volume of this cylinder?

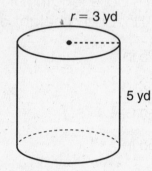

   r = 3 yd

   5 yd

   A. 141.3 yd^3

   B. 197.8 yd^3

   C. 282.6 yd^3

   D. 329.7 yd^3

8. What is the perimeter of this polygon?

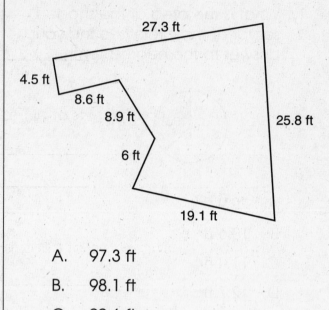

   27.3 ft

   4.5 ft

   8.6 ft

   8.9 ft

   25.8 ft

   6 ft

   19.1 ft

   A. 97.3 ft

   B. 98.1 ft

   C. 99.6 ft

   D. 100.2 ft

9. A triangle has an area of 34 m^2. If you double the base length and height of the triangle, what will be the area of the triangle?

   A. 68 m^2

   B. 136 m^2

   C. 272 m^2

   D. 544 m^2

10. Kendall is going to draw a rectangle that has the same area as the parallelogram.

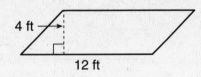

4 ft

12 ft

What are two possible sets of dimensions for the rectangle?

_____

_____

11. What is the surface area of this cylinder?

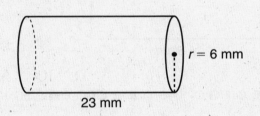

r = 6 mm

23 mm

A. 866.64 mm²

B. 979.68 mm²

C. 1,017.36 mm²

D. 1,092.72 mm²

12. The following solid is a cube.

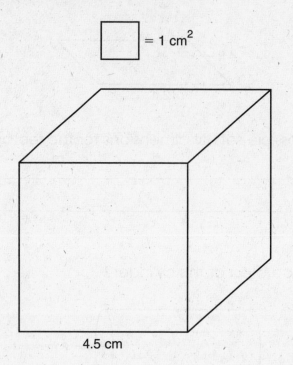

= 1 cm^2

4.5 cm

Estimate the surface area of the cube and explain the strategy you used.

_____

_____

_____

_____

_____

In the box below, calculate the actual surface area of the cube.

SA = _____

Unit 5

Data Analysis and Probability

Data analysis and probability are used in more ways than you might think. Farmers may consider data about rainfall, temperature, and yield when planting crops. City planners look at traffic data when they think about building new roads. Data are even used in some situations to help determine probability. Scientists often use data from experiments to determine the probability of certain events. A baseball player's batting average is the experimental probability that the player will get a hit. Other times, probability is based on purely mathematical odds. For example, when you flip a coin, you know the theoretical probability of it landing heads up is always 50%.

In this unit, you will describe data using mean, median, mode, and range. You will construct and interpret different graphical representations of data. You will also compare theoretical and experimental probability.

In This Unit

Statistics and
   Data Analysis

Probability

Lesson 13

Statistics and Data Analysis

In this lesson, you will describe and compare data sets using measures of central tendency and range. You will also construct and interpret charts and graphs to analyze data.

Measures of Central Tendency

To understand how to interpret data, it is important to know about the mean, median, and mode of a data set. You should also be familiar with **outliers**—values in a data set widely separated from the main cluster of values in the set.

Mean

The **mean** is the sum of the numbers in a data set divided by how many numbers there are in the set. The mean is often called the "average."

$$\text{mean} = \frac{\textbf{sum of the numbers}}{\textbf{how many numbers}}$$

Example

A bookcase has 5 shelves with 38, 42, 47, 36, and 37 books on them. What is the mean number of books per shelf?

First, add the 5 numbers.

$$38 + 42 + 47 + 36 + 37 = 200$$

Now, substitute the numbers into the formula and calculate the mean.

$$\text{mean} = \frac{\text{sum of the numbers}}{\text{how many numbers}}$$

$$= \frac{200}{5}$$

$$= 40$$

The mean number of books per shelf is 40.

Median

The **median** is the **middle** number in a data set arranged from least to greatest (or greatest to least).

 **Example**

The following list shows the number of customers who ordered pie at Ma & Pa's Diner each day last week.

8, 11, 7, 20, 13, 7, 10

What is the median number of customers who ordered pie?

Arrange the numbers in order from least to greatest. Find the middle number.

7, 7, 8, **10**, 11, 13, 20

The median number of customers who ordered pie is 10.

When a data set has an even number of numbers, find the two middle numbers. Add the two middle numbers and divide by 2 to find the median.

Example

What is the median of the following data set?

33, 17, 29, 26, 41, 22

Arrange the numbers in order from least to greatest. Find the two middle numbers.

17, 22, **26, 29**, 33, 41

Add the two middle numbers and divide by 2.

$$\frac{26 + 29}{2} = \frac{55}{2} = 27.5$$

The median of the data set is 27.5.

Mode

The **mode** is the number that appears **most often** in a data set.

 **Example**

Steve played nine holes of golf and shot the following scores.

4, 5, 4, 6, 3, 7, 4, 5, 4

What is the mode of the scores?

Find the score that appears most often.

4, 5, **4**, 6, 3, 7, **4**, 5, **4**

The mode of the scores is 4.

In some data sets, there might be two modes, or if no number appears more than once, no mode at all.

Example

What is the mode of the following data set?

22, 35, 18, 22, 20, 35, 32, 24

Find the number that appears most often.

22, **35**, 18, **22**, 20, **35**, 32, 24

This data set has **two modes:** 22 and 35.

Example

What is the mode of the following data set?

45, 37, 48, 27, 31, 35, 102, 30

Find the number that appears most often.

Each number appears only once.

This data set has **no mode**.

Practice

1. Find the mean, median, mode, and any possible outliers of the following data set.

   17, 32, 37, 21, 28, 32, 83, 20, 27

   mean: _____ median: _____ mode(s): _____ outlier(s): _____

Directions: Use the following information to answer Numbers 2 through 6. Round your answers to the nearest tenth.

The following table shows the final score for each game the Browns played in the 2002 football season.

2002 Browns' Results

Browns	39	20	31	13	21	3	34	24	20	27	24	6	21	23	14	24
Opponents	40	7	28	16	26	17	17	21	23	20	15	13	20	28	13	16

2. Find the mean number of points scored by the Browns and by their opponents.

   Browns: _____ opponents: _____

3. Who had a higher mean, the Browns or their opponents? _____

4. Find the median number of points scored by the Browns and by their opponents.

   Browns: _____ opponents: _____

5. Who had a higher median, the Browns or their opponents? _____

6. Find the mode number of points scored by the Browns and by their opponents.

   Browns: _____ opponents: _____

Range

The **range** is the difference between the smallest number, the **minimum**, and the largest number, the **maximum**, in a data set.

 **Example**

What is the range of the following data set?

49, 23, 73, 91, 88

Find the minimum (23) and the maximum (91). Subtract the minimum from the maximum:

91 − 23 = 68

The range of the data set is 68.

 **Practice**

Directions: Use the following information to answer Numbers 1 through 4.

Bart and Lisa received the following scores on six math quizzes.

Bart: 93, 88, 95, 97, 90, 85

Lisa: 90, 79, 86, 94, 99, 89

1. Find the minimum of Bart's and Lisa's scores.

Bart: _____ Lisa: _____

2. Find the maximum of Bart's and Lisa's scores.

Bart: _____ Lisa: _____

3. Find the range of Bart's and Lisa's scores.

Bart: _____ Lisa: _____

4. Who had a wider range of scores, Bart or Lisa? _____

182

Data Analysis

Tables and graphs are good ways of organizing and displaying data for analysis.

Frequency tables

A **frequency table** organizes information by using tally marks to count how many of something there are.

 Example

> The following frequency table shows the favorite season of each student in Mr. Fletcher's class.

Favorite Seasons

Season	Tally	Number of Students
Winter	ЖНТ	5
Spring	ЖНТ III	8
Summer	ЖНТ ЖНТ III	13
Autumn	III	3

Practice

Directions: Use the information from the frequency table above to answer Numbers 1 through 4.

1. How many students chose autumn as their favorite season? _____

2. What season was the favorite of exactly 8 students? _____

3. How many more students chose summer as their favorite season than chose winter?

   _____

4. How many students are represented by the frequency table? _____

5. Some sixth graders from all over Ohio were asked randomly which neighboring state was closest to their home town. The following list shows the results.

Michigan, Indiana, West Virginia, West Virginia, Pennsylvania, Pennsylvania, Michigan, Kentucky, Indiana, Indiana, Pennsylvania, Kentucky, Indiana, West Virginia, Michigan, Indiana, Kentucky, West Virginia, Indiana, Pennsylvania, Michigan, West Virginia, Indiana, West Virginia, Indiana, Indiana, Pennsylvania, West Virginia, Kentucky, Indiana, Indiana, West Virginia, Kentucky, Kentucky, Michigan, West Virginia, Pennsylvania, West Virginia, Kentucky, Pennsylvania, Indiana, Michigan

Display the data from the list in a frequency table.

Closest Bordering State to Home

State	Tally	Number of Students
Pennsylvania		
West Virginia		
Kentucky		
Indiana		
Michigan		

Directions: Use the frequency table you constructed in Number 5 to answer Numbers 6 through 8.

6. What state was closest to the home town of exactly 10 students?

_____

7. Which two states were closest to an equal number of students?

A. West Virginia and Indiana

B. Michigan and Pennsylvania

C. Kentucky and Pennsylvania

D. West Virginia and Kentucky

8. How many more sixth graders named Indiana the closest state than Michigan?

A. 2

B. 5

C. 6

D. 11

Bar graphs

A **bar graph** is usually used to compare amounts of similar things.

Example

Mrs. Mable's class had to write a report on their favorite U.S. president from Ohio. The following bar graph shows the number of reports on each president.

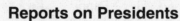
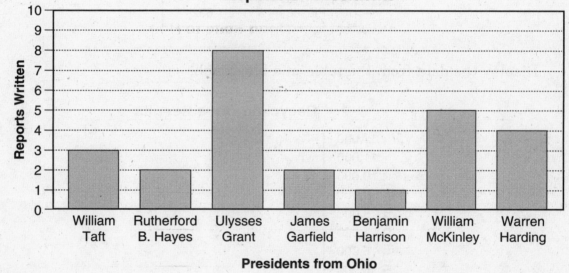

Reports on Presidents

Presidents from Ohio

Practice

Directions: Use the bar graph above to answer Numbers 1 through 5.

1. Which president was chosen by most students? _____

2. How many more reports were on Harding than Harrison? _____

3. How many students are in Mrs. Mable's class? _____

4. Which president was the topic of 20% of all reports? _____

5. Which two presidents were chosen by the same number of students?

_____

6. Lincoln Elementary School has a recycling drive every year. The following table shows the results of last year's recycling drive.

Recycling Drive Results

Item	Amount (in pounds)
Glass	2,115
Metal	7,228
Paper	11,950
Plastic	832

Display the data from the table in a bar graph.

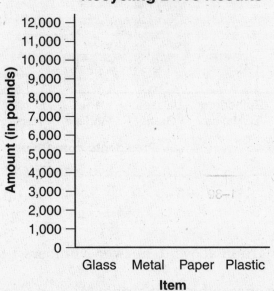

Directions: Use the table and the bar graph you constructed in Number 6 to answer Numbers 7 and 8.

7. What item did the school collect the most pounds of?

   A. glass
   B. metal
   C. paper
   D. plastic

8. **About** how much did the school collect altogether for the entire year?

   A. 20,000 pounds
   B. 22,000 pounds
   C. 24,000 pounds
   D. 26,000 pounds

Histograms

A **histogram** is a type of bar graph that is used to show continuous data. The horizontal axis is labeled using intervals. A histogram uses bars that are always vertical and connected to each other. The height of each bar represents the frequency.

Example

After 5 hours, the first 25 participants of the 100-km bike tour at the National Popcorn Festival had traveled the following distances from the starting point.

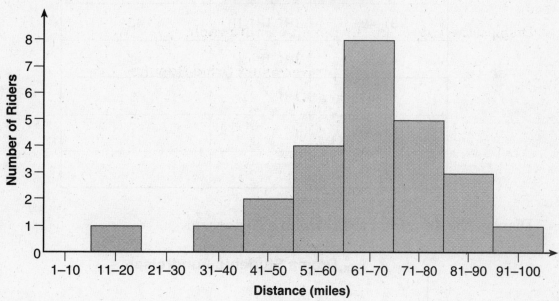

Bike Tour Distances

Practice

Directions: Use the histogram above to answer Numbers 1 through 4.

1. How many people rode more than 70 km? _____

2. In what interval does the median distance lie? _____

3. In what interval is there a possible outlier? _____

4. Does the histogram appear to be symmetric? Explain.

   _____

   _____

5. The drama students at North Woods High School sold candy bars to raise money for new costumes. The following table shows the amount of money the students were able to raise.

Drama Students Fundraiser

Money Raised ($)	Tally	Number of Students
0–10	II	2
11–20	IIII IIII	9
21–30	IIII IIII IIII	14
31–40	IIII IIII III	13
41–50	IIII III	8
51–60	IIII	5
61–70	I	1
71–80	I	1

Display the data from the table in a histogram.

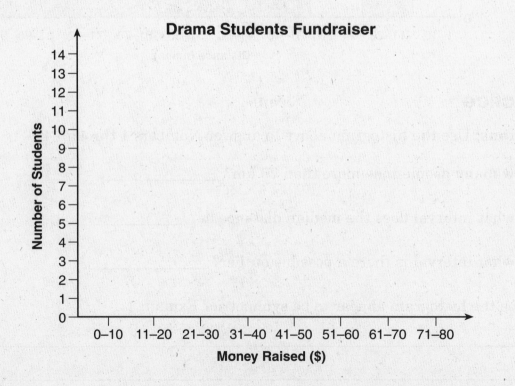

Directions: Use the table and the histogram you constructed in Number 5 to answer Numbers 6 through 10.

6. How many students raised an amount that falls within the lowest interval?

    A. 1
    B. 2
    C. 9
    D. 14

7. How many students raised more than $30?

    A. 4
    B. 13
    C. 25
    D. 28

8. In what two intervals are there an equal number of students?

    A. 0–10 and 11–20
    B. 11–20 and 41–50
    C. 21–30 and 31–40
    D. 61–70 and 71–80

9. In what interval are there the most students?

    A. 11–20
    B. 21–30
    C. 51–60
    D. 71–80

10. In what interval does the median number of students lie?

    A. 11–20
    B. 21–30
    C. 31–40
    D. 41–50

Line graphs

A **line graph** shows increases and/or decreases in data. Line graphs are usually best for showing trends or changes in something over a period of time.

Example

A florist kept track of sales of scarlet carnations, Ohio's state flower, from July 15 through July 24. She made the following line graph to show how many scarlet carnations were sold in arrangements during those ten days.

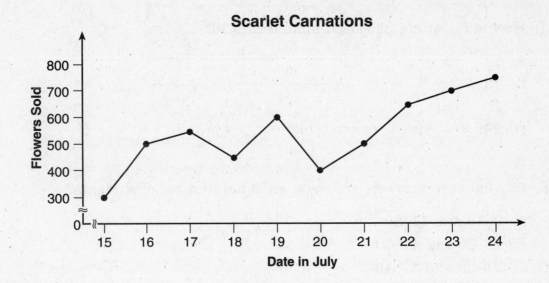

Practice

Directions: Use the line graph above to answer Numbers 1 through 4.

1. How many carnations were sold on July 19? _____

2. On what day were over 700 carnations sold? _____

3. On what two days were the same number of carnations sold?

   _____

4. On how many days were the carnation sales lower than on the previous day?

   _____

5. Nate made the following table to show his fastest time each year in the 400-meter dash.

400-Meter Dash

Age (in years)	Time (in seconds)
13	65.9
14	62.3
15	57.2
16	54.6
17	52.5
18	51.2

Display the data from the table in a line graph.

400-Meter Dash

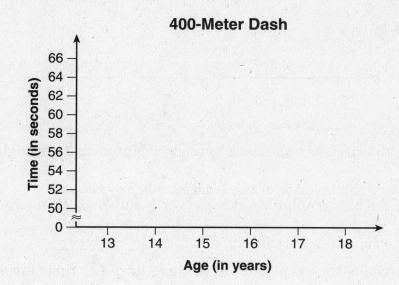

Directions: Use the table and the line graph you constructed in Number 5 to answer Numbers 6 and 7.

6. At what age did Nate have the largest decrease in time from the previous year?

   A. 14
   B. 15
   C. 16
   D. 17

7. Which is the **best** prediction of what Nate's fastest time will be when he is 19 years old?

   A. 46.9 seconds
   B. 48.6 seconds
   C. 50.4 seconds
   D. 52.5 seconds

Circle graphs

A **circle graph** is divided into sections to represent portions of a data set. The sections of a circle graph add up to 100%.

 **Example**

Zoe surveyed her classmates to find out what their favorite fruit juices are. She made the following circle graph to show her results.

Favorite Fruit Juices

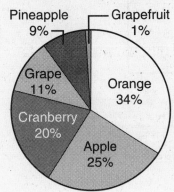

Practice

Directions: Use the circle graph above to answer Numbers 1 through 4.

1. Which juice was the favorite of the least number of people?

   _____

2. What percentage of the people surveyed chose grape as their favorite juice?

   _____

3. Which juice was the favorite of the same number of people as pineapple and apple combined?

   _____

4. For every 100 people surveyed, how many chose cranberry as their favorite juice?

   _____

5. The following frequency table shows the post-season hits that Dwight had during his career.

Dwight's Hits

Type of Hit	Tally	Number
Single	⌶⌶⌶⌶⌶ ⌶⌶⌶⌶⌶ ⌶⌶⌶⌶⌶	15
Double	⌶⌶⌶⌶⌶ II	7
Triple	I	1
Home Run	IIII	4

Display the data from the table in a circle graph. Round percents to the nearest tenth.

Dwight's Hits

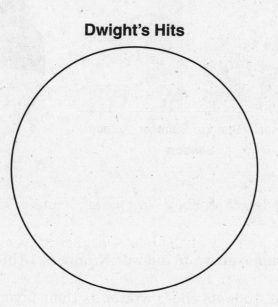

Directions: Use the frequency table and the circle graph you constructed in Number 5 to answer Numbers 6 and 7.

6. What percentage of Dwight's hits were home runs?

   A. 3.7%

   B. 14.8%

   C. 25.9%

   D. 55.6%

7. What type of hit did Dwight get most of the time?

   A. single

   B. double

   C. triple

   D. home run

Comparing Graphs

Sometimes you can use more than one type of graph to display the same data. You can compare different graphical representations of the same data to find out which one is better to use in a certain situation.

Example

Mr. Fletcher used the data from the frequency table on page 183 to make the following bar graph and circle graph of the data. The percentages on the circle graph were rounded to the nearest percent.

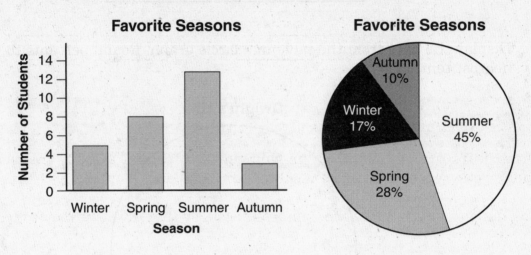

Practice

Directions: Use the graphs above to answer Numbers 1 through 3.

1. What percent of the students chose winter as their favorite season?

   _____

2. How many students chose summer as their favorite season? _____

3. Explain why you would use each graph in different situations.

   _____

   _____

   _____

Representations of data

When you want to display data, you need to decide what representation will work best for that particular data set. The following table shows the purposes of different representations of data.

Representations and Purposes

Representation	Purpose of Data
Frequency table	organizing numbers
Bar graph	comparing amounts
Histogram	comparing amounts of continuous data
Line graph	showing change over time
Circle graph	comparing parts of a whole

 **Practice**

Directions: For each situation in Numbers 1 through 5, identify the most appropriate representation to display the given data.

1. You want to compare the amounts of money that different movies earned.

   _____

2. You want to show how the attendance at a basketball game rose or fell during an entire basketball season.

   _____

3. You want to show the percentages of the total number of T-shirts sold that were blue, yellow, or white.

   _____

4. You want to organize a large list of numbers that represent the numbers of books students in your class read last year.

   _____

5. You want to show the number of people from different age groups that attended a movie.

   _____

Achievement Practice

Directions: Use the following circle graph to answer questions 1 and 2.

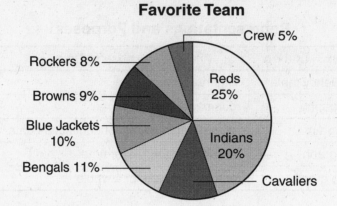

Favorite Team

1. What sport team is represented on $\frac{1}{4}$ of the graph?

   A. Rockers

   B. Indians

   C. Crew

   D. Reds

2. What percent chose the Indians as their favorite team?

   A. 5%

   B. 10%

   C. 20%

   D. 25%

Directions: Use the following histogram to answer questions 3 and 4.

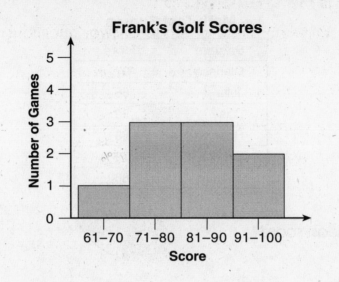

3. How many times did Frank score higher than 80?

   A. 2

   B. 3

   C. 4

   D. 5

4. In what interval does the median score lie?

   A. 91–100

   B. 81–90

   C. 71–80

   D. 61–70

Directions: Use the following table to answer questions 5 through 7.

Math Test Scores

Student	Score
Clarissa	97
Julia	86
Luis	92
Roberto	88
Sandra	79
Thomas	86

5. What is the mean score?

   A. 87

   B. 88

   C. 90

   D. 92

6. What is the mode of the scores?

   A. 79

   B. 86

   C. 88

   D. 97

7. What is the median of the scores?

   A. 85

   B. 86

   C. 87

   D. 88

8. Amy is an assistant coach for the girls' track team. She recorded the times the girls ran in the one-mile run. She wants to group the times into intervals and graph the data to see how many girls ran times in each interval. Which representation would be best for Amy to use?

   A. histogram

   B. bar graph

   C. line graph

   D. circle graph

9. The following data set has an outlier of 60.

   10, 28, 14, 13, 24, 60, 19

   What is the mean of the data set with and without the outlier? Show your work.

   with: _____

   without: _____

Directions: Use the following line graph to answer questions 10 and 11.

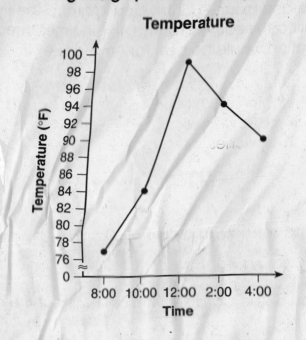

Temperature

10. When did the largest increase in temperature occur?

    A.   between 8:00 and 10:00

    B.   between 10:00 and 12:00

    C.   between 12:00 and 2:00

    D.   between 2:00 and 4:00

11. Give the median and the range of the five temperatures recorded.

    median: _____

    range: _____

12. Miss Parker's class is having a picnic. The menu is sandwiches, fruit, potato salad, pretzels, and desserts. Each student volunteered to bring one of the menu items. The following list shows the items the students volunteered to bring:

> sandwiches, fruit, fruit, potato salad, dessert, sandwiches, pretzels, dessert, fruit, potato salad, fruit, sandwiches, dessert, potato salad, pretzels, sandwiches, dessert, fruit, sandwiches, pretzels, dessert, sandwiches, sandwiches, potato salad, dessert, fruit, dessert

Display the data from the list in a frequency table.

Picnic Items

Item	Tally	Number of Students
Sandwiches		
Fruit		
Potato Salad		
Pretzels		
Dessert		

Display the data from the frequency table in a bar graph.

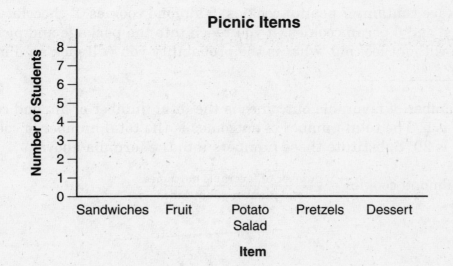

Picnic Items

Lesson 14

Probability

Probability is the chance that an event will occur. In this lesson, you will review ways of finding the theoretical probability or experimental probability that an event will occur.

Theoretical Probability (Simple Events)

Theoretical probability is based on mathematical reasoning. A **simple event** is an event that has a single outcome. The theoretical probability of a simple event can be found using the following formula.

$$P(\text{event}) = \frac{\text{number of favorable outcomes}}{\text{total number of outcomes}}$$

Probability can be expressed as a fraction in lowest terms or a decimal between 0 and 1. An event that has a probability less than $\frac{1}{2}$ is an **unlikely event**. An event that has a probability greater than $\frac{1}{2}$ is a **likely event**. An event can also have a probability of 0 or 1. An event that has a probability of 0 is an **impossible event**. An event that has a probability of 1 is a **certain event**.

Example

A package contains 7 peanut cookies, 5 almond cookies, 2 chocolate-chip cookies, and 6 pecan cookies. If you reach into the package and pick a cookie without looking, what is the probability you will pick an almond cookie?

The number of favorable outcomes is the total number of almond cookies, which is 5. The total number of outcomes is the total number of cookies, which is 20. Substitute these numbers into the formula above.

$$P(\text{almond cookie}) = \frac{\text{number of favorable outcomes}}{\text{total number of outcomes}}$$

$$= \frac{5}{20}$$

$$= \frac{1}{4}$$

The probability of picking an almond cookie is $\frac{1}{4}$.

Practice

1. An octahedron (8-sided solid) with sides numbered 1 through 8 is rolled. What is the probability of rolling a 6?

   _____

2. If you have to guess the answer to a true or false question, what is the probability you will answer it correctly?

   _____

3. The 26 different letters of the alphabet are written on cards, one letter per card, and placed into a bag. What is the probability of drawing the letter M without looking?

   _____

4. Each week, Mrs. Rogers randomly chooses one student in her class to clean the chalkboard erasers. If there are 16 girls and 10 boys in her class, what is the probability of her choosing a boy to clean the erasers?

   _____

5. Maya's cat hid her 5 kittens behind the living room couch, 2 are black and 3 are white. If Maya pulls a kitten from behind the couch without looking, what is the probability that the kitten will be white?

   _____

6. Eric has a bag with 20 jelly beans left in it: 5 are orange, 7 are red, and the rest are purple. What is the probability of pulling a purple jelly bean out of the bag without looking?

   A. $\frac{1}{3}$

   B. $\frac{2}{5}$

   C. $\frac{3}{5}$

   D. $\frac{2}{3}$

7. Tara has 24 bottle caps in a bag: 4 are red, 8 are white, 3 are orange, and 9 are yellow. If she pulls a bottle cap out of the bag without looking, what color has the highest probability of being pulled?

   A. red
   B. white
   C. orange
   D. yellow

Experimental Probability

Experimental probability is based on an actual experiment. Experimental probability can be used to test predictions. The experimental probability of an event is the chance that the event actually occurs when a number of trials is performed. The experimental probability of an event can be found using the following formula.

$$P(\text{event}) = \frac{\text{number of actual outcomes}}{\text{number of trials}}$$

Example

The following table shows the outcomes from tossing a coin 10 times. What is the experimental probability of tossing heads?

Toss	1	2	3	4	5	6	7	8	9	10
Outcome	H	H	T	T	H	T	T	H	T	T

The number of actual outcomes is the number of times heads was tossed, which is 4. The number of trials performed is 10. Substitute these numbers into the formula above.

$$P(\text{heads}) = \frac{\text{number of actual outcomes}}{\text{number of trials}}$$

$$= \frac{4}{10}$$

$$= \frac{2}{5}$$

The experimental probability of tossing heads is $\frac{2}{5}$.

An experiment is usually performed to test a theoretical probability. The theoretical probability of tossing heads on a coin is $\frac{1}{2}$. In the example above, the experimental probability of tossing heads is $\frac{2}{5}$. As more trials are performed in an experiment, the experimental probability should get closer to the theoretical probability.

TIP: The experimental probability changes with every new trial you perform.

Practice

Directions: For Numbers 1 through 4, use your experimental results to test a theoretical probability.

1. If you roll a number cube once, what is the theoretical probability of rolling each number from 1 through 6?

    P(1): _____   P(3): _____   P(5): _____

    P(2): _____   P(4): _____   P(6): _____

2. Roll a number cube 60 times and record your results in the following table.

Outcome	Number of Times
1	
2	
3	
4	
5	
6	

3. What is your experimental probability of rolling each number from 1 through 6?

    exp P(1): _____   exp P(3): _____   exp P(5): _____

    exp P(2): _____   exp P(4): _____   exp P(6): _____

4. How does each of your experimental probabilities compare to the theoretical probability?

    _____

    _____

    _____

Directions: For Numbers 5 through 8, use your experimental results to test a theoretical probability.

5. If you flip a coin in the air once, what is the theoretical probability it will land heads up? What is the theoretical probability it will land tails up?

   P(heads): _____ P(tails): _____

6. Flip a coin in the air 20 times and record your results in the following table.

Outcome	Number of Times
Heads (H)	
Tails (T)	

7. What is your experimental probability of a head and a tail landing up?

   exp P(H): _____   exp P(T): _____

8. How does each of your experimental probabilities compare to the theoretical probability?

   _____

   _____

   _____

9. Logan rolled a number cube 30 times. What is the best prediction for the number of times he rolled a 6?

   A. 1
   B. 5
   C. 6
   D. 10

Outcomes

Tree diagrams and lists are used to show all the possible outcomes of an event in an organized way. The fundamental counting principle is used to find the number of possible outcomes of an event. Once you find the number of possible outcomes, you can determine the probability of an event occurring.

Tree diagrams

Tree diagrams use branches to show all possible outcomes of an event.

 **Example**

When a coin is tossed once, there are two possible outcomes: heads (H) or tails (T). The following tree diagram shows the possible outcomes when a coin is tossed three times.

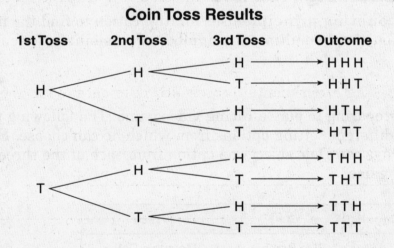

There are 8 possible outcomes when a coin is tossed three times.

Since there are 8 possible outcomes, the probability of any one outcome occurring is $\frac{1}{8}$.

Lists

Instead of drawing a tree diagram, you can simply use a list to show all the possible outcomes.

Example

The following list shows the possible ways of answering three true (T) or false (F) questions.

TTT	TFT	FTT	FFT
TTF	TFF	FTF	FFF

The list shows that there are 8 possible ways of answering three true or false questions.

Fundamental Counting Principle

The **fundamental counting principle** uses multiplication to find the number of possible outcomes. You simply multiply the number of possibilities for each choice.

Example

Dale was preparing to play a racing video game. The following table shows the different setting options from which he can choose. How many different ways can Dale select one option from each of the three categories to play the game?

Players	Car	Track
1	Blue Bomber	Mountain Paths
2	Red Racer	Ocean Side
4	Yellow Yeller	Urban Raceway
	Green Ghost	

There are 3 choices for number of players, 4 choices for a car, and 3 choices for a track.

$$3 \cdot 4 \cdot 3 = 36$$

There are 36 different race combinations from which Dale can choose.

Practice

Directions: For Numbers 1 and 2, draw a tree diagram to show the possible outcomes. Then write how many possible outcomes there are.

1. Melissa will find all possible 3-digit numbers with either a 1 or 2 in the hundreds place; either a 3, 4, or 6 in the tens place; and a 7, 8, 9, or 0 in the ones place. How many of these 3-digit numbers are there?

2. There are 3 offices for a school's student council: president, secretary, and treasurer. The candidates for president are Merv (M), Stacey (S), and Johanna (J). The candidates for secretary are Vince (V) and Rochelle (R). The candidates for treasurer are Bill (B) and Dave (D). How many possible ways are there to fill these positions?

3. The bank is offering 200 free checks to customers who open an account. There is a choice from the following colors, scenes, and text styles.

   color: blue, green, brown

   scene: none, animals

   text style: standard, script

Make a list to show the different ways a customer can order checks.

4. The following table shows the choices a store has for delivery.

Day	Time	Truck Driver
Monday	8 A.M.–11 A.M.	Frank
Tuesday	11 A.M.–3 P.M.	Mike
Wednesday	3 P.M.–6 P.M.	Jim
Thursday		Sue

How many different combinations of delivery day, time, and driver are available from this store?

_____

5. The snack bar has 3 types of juice, 4 types of sandwiches, and 2 types of chips. How many different ways can you choose one of each food type?

   A. 12

   B. 18

   C. 24

   D. 48

6. There are 5 possible paths to get from the ranger's station to the pond and 2 possible paths from the pond to the cave. How many paths are there from the ranger's station to the cave by way of the pond?

   A. 2

   B. 5

   C. 7

   D. 10

Achievement Practice

Directions: Use the following information to answer questions 1 and 2.

Ellis flipped a quarter into the air 50 times. Heads landed up 28 times and tails landed up 22 times.

1. What is the experimental probability of tails landing up?

    A. $\frac{11}{25}$

    B. $\frac{1}{2}$

    C. $\frac{14}{25}$

    D. $\frac{14}{14}$

2. If Ellis flips the coin another 50 times and adds his results to those he already has, what should happen?

    A. The experimental probability of heads landing up should be closer to the theoretical probability.

    B. The experimental probability of heads landing up should be farther away from the theoretical probability.

    C. The experimental probability of heads landing up should be exactly the same as the theoretical probability.

    D. The experimental probability of heads landing up should be equal to 1.

Directions: Use the following information to answer questions 3 and 4.

Eight green marbles, 7 red marbles, 6 blue marbles, and 3 silver marbles are dropped into a jar.

3. What is the probability of picking a blue marble from the jar without looking?

    A. $\frac{1}{6}$

    B. $\frac{1}{4}$

    C. $\frac{3}{11}$

    D. $\frac{3}{8}$

4. What is the probability of picking a marble that is **not** silver from the jar without looking?

    A. $\frac{1}{8}$

    B. $\frac{13}{24}$

    C. $\frac{3}{4}$

    D. $\frac{7}{8}$

5. Luis rolled a number cube 12 times and recorded the following results.

    6, 3, 1, 1, 6, 5, 4, 2, 3, 3, 1, 3

    What is the experimental probability of rolling a 3?

    A. $\frac{1}{4}$

    B. $\frac{1}{3}$

    C. $\frac{5}{12}$

    D. $\frac{1}{2}$

6. Mr. and Mrs. Wilcox are selecting their vacation destination by spinning the following spinner.

    What is the probability that they will vacation in Akron?

    A. $\frac{1}{3}$

    B. $\frac{3}{14}$

    C. $\frac{1}{8}$

    D. $\frac{1}{24}$

Directions: Allison wants to buy a folder and a notebook from the school bookstore. The following table shows the store's current stock of folders and notebooks. Use it to answer questions 7 and 8.

Color	Folders	Notebooks
Red	3	0
Yellow	2	4
Green	1	3
Blue	4	5
TOTAL	10	12

7. If Allison picks a folder without looking, what is the probability that it will be yellow?

    A. $\frac{1}{4}$

    B. $\frac{1}{5}$

    C. $\frac{1}{6}$

    D. $\frac{1}{10}$

8. If Allison picks a notebook without looking, what is the probability that it will **not** be yellow?

    A. 0

    B. $\frac{1}{3}$

    C. $\frac{2}{3}$

    D. $\frac{3}{4}$

9. Sara can choose from 4 guards, 7 forwards, and 5 centers for her three-person basketball team. How many different teams can she make if she chooses a guard, forward, and center? Show your work.

Notes

Notes

Notes

Notes